I0796192

A little guide to

# Crystals

# A little guide to Crystals

Harnessing natural energies for wellbeing

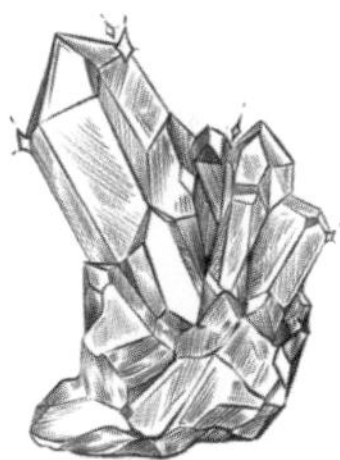

Megan Kaye

AMMONITE
PRESS

# Contents



**Safety tips**

Don't start a fire! A crystal can refract light to a fine point, especially if it's transparent, and it can focus the sun's rays like a magnifying glass. Use common sense, be aware of where the light falls in your home and keep them away from anything flammable. You can safely make an 'elixir' by putting a crystal next to water, setting an intention and letting its energies charge the water, which you then drink. Some practitioners advise putting the crystal in the water (or even your mouth), but this is strongly discouraged: some crystals can have potentially toxic soluble elements, and pathogens might lurk in their nooks and crannies. For the same reason it's always wise to wash your hands after handling crystals, as some contain minerals such as copper and aluminium that aren't good to ingest. The odds are against you taking in a high enough dose to do you any harm – and you should never grind the gems to powder and swallow or inhale them – but a bit of basic health and safety can only support your practice. Unlike soluble crystals, your skin is definitely washable, so err on the side of caution.

# The crystals

# What is a Crystal?

*Pick up a crystal* and you'll be holding magic in your hand. A gleam of colour will delight your eyes, but you'll also be cradling in your palm a piece of ancient history: a creation forged by the Earth itself.

Put simply, a crystal is a stone where the beauty of its ordered structure is present right down to its molecules. The word 'crystal' comes from the ancient Greek *cryo*, meaning 'ice', and in this itself we can see the significance of these little things: a flowing power frozen into solidity.

## Beneath the lens

What distinguishes crystals from other rocks and minerals is that they have what is known as 'lattice' – an arrangement that duplicates itself in three dimensions in a perfectly regular pattern. The crystal itself may not look regular to the naked eye, of course, but you could put it under a microscope and see the design at its cellular level. You could even put two crystals that looked completely different in colour and opacity side by side, and there, magnified, would be the geologic DNA that unites them. That's the science.

## Ancient amulets

Crystals have been prized for their beauty and healing powers throughout human history. Amulets of amber as old as ten thousand years have been discovered in Britain. Palaeolithic graves in Belgium and Switzerland have been found that contained jet beads. Ancient Sumerians practised crystal healing in Mesopotamia, and in Sinai, malachite was mined six thousand years ago. Ancient Egyptians would wear lapis lazuli, carnelian and turquoise to ward off bad influences.

Although the Christian Church banned the use of amulets in 355 CE, priests continued to prize gemstones in their ceremonial gear. In the Renaissance, scholars believed them to have 'virtues' – for example, the Italian natural philosopher Girolamo Cardano (1501–1576) argued that gems held a 'correspondence' with the celestial bodies he believed held sway over the terrestrial world.

## Today's approach

Modern crystal treatments can vary from practitioner to practitioner, but regardless, you should always listen to your own instincts. This book will give you a better understanding of what those instincts are telling you.

As we use crystals, we talk about energies that resonate with our own life force energy – what is known as *qi* in traditional Chinese medicine, and what the Hindu and Buddhist beliefs are speaking of when describing the chakras (see pages 20–25). What we mean is that the universe is made of energy and so are you – and if you can find ways to manage its flow, your life force, you can direct your spirit, cleanse your mind and tune up your body.

Experiment and pay attention to your experiences, and when you find a positive channel, follow where it leads. You never know what you might unlock if you approach with curiosity.

# How Crystals Form

*We live on a spinning globe* of molten rock adorned with crust and life. It's an astonishing thought when you stop to consider it; the power under your feet right now is titanic. When you look at a crystal, you're seeing the slow, dynamic metamorphosis of that power made into a solid object.

## Natural gemstones

The name of that blazing liquid at the centre of our world is magma. It's always moving, and sometimes it reaches a place where it cools and forms crystals. Consider what happens to water when it cools enough: it sets into a solid object, ice, where all the molecules within it form into a regular structure. Essentially, that's what happens in the creation of crystals too.

There are other ways crystals can be formed naturally. Molecules dissolved in liquid can coalesce around a single grain, ordering themselves into a lattice structure as the liquid dissolves – which is how you get the crystalline sea salt.

The common factor is that the atoms line themselves up in a particular order. However, when it comes to the crystals we use for healing, it's usually the ones created by cooling rock: you're looking at 'frozen' magma.

## Dating a crystal

There's a science called 'geochronology' that can determine how old a rock is based on its exact composition. If it's got the structure that a particular known geological event would have created, that's how old it is. Think of how we date felled trees based on the number of rings inside their trunk, comparing the years of fast and slow growth to what we know about the historical years of warm and cold weather – and then imagine that on a scale of eons. That's what crystals contain. These are ancient artefacts sculpted by our planet: there are zircons from Australia almost 4.3 billion years old, almost as old as the Earth itself.

Imagine a warm, humid room; the world outside is cold. A droplet of water forms itself on the window. Think of that in geologic time. A crystal is a piece of our planet shaped on a scale that staggers the human imagination.

## Lab gemstones

With relatively recent technology it's become possible to create gemstones in laboratories. They were first manufactured in the 19th century, with the first success being the creation of a facet-quality ruby. Nowadays plenty of synthetic crystals are made for industrial uses such as communications technology, microelectronics and lasers. These are truly useful items.

Are they any good for crystal healing? Some say that because they don't partake of ancient processes, they don't carry the same resonance. Others are more flexible. There are definite advantages to synthetic gemstones, including being a lot cheaper. They're not 'fake' in the sense of being a different substance to their natural equivalents: physically, they're identical – they have the same atoms in the same lattice, following the exact same recipe the Earth invented. And there's an ethical argument in their favour: mining conditions can be terrible and synthetic crystals don't partake in that.

In the end it's your own choice. We always cleanse crystals and bring our own energy to them, so if you feel you can work with synthetic ones, then go for it. There's nothing synthetic about the self as you work with them, after all.

# Internal Structures

*When we talk about crystals* we talk a lot about energies, so let's talk about the most fundamental building block of the universe: the atom. Because when it comes down to it, an atom is a powerhouse.

## Atomic energy

If you look at a diagram of an atom, you'll probably see spheres stuck together, which makes it look something like a child's toy made of round blocks. In reality, though, most of an atom is empty space. While there isn't exactly a solid object, there is a bundle of energy moving so fast that it *becomes* what we think of as solid.

An atom is made up of three subatomic particles, and it's how their charge interacts that makes it what it is. At the centre is a cluster of protons and neutrons – the former being particles with a positive electric charge, and the latter with no charge, hence 'neutral'. (The one exception is the hydrogen atom, the simplest of all, which has one proton and no neutrons.) You can think of this positively charged central cluster as a planet, and around it orbits a cloud of tiny, negatively charged moons known as electrons. The difference is what keeps them circulating: while the Moon orbits the Earth because of Earth's gravitational pull, what drives the electrons is electricity.

If you've ever watched two ends of a magnet snap together, you've seen this force in action. Magnets attract at their opposite ends – what we refer to as their north pole and south pole. With protons and electrons, it's the opposite forces of positive and negative charge. The attraction of the nucleus keeps the electrons

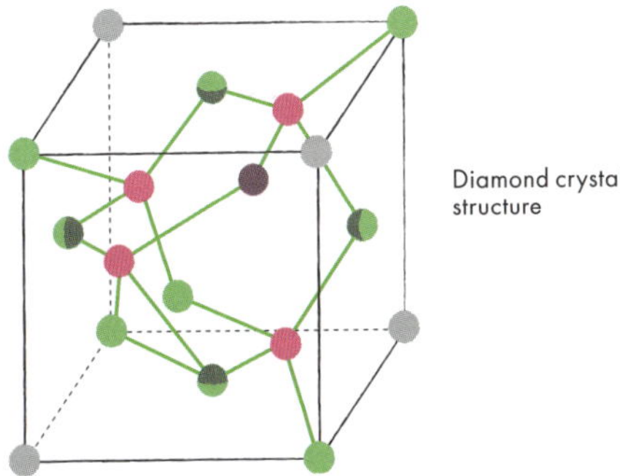

Diamond crystal structure

spinning, and it's the different composition of protons, neutrons and electrons that makes up the different atoms.

What does this have to do with crystal healing? Well, it's the energy that we can feel when approaching a crystal that we find appealing, but to understand this, we need to know that the crystal – and we ourselves – are essentially energy in motion.

## Structural patterns

So, we now know that atoms are like little planets with orbiting moons. The question is: how do crystals form the orderly constellations that make up a lattice structure? The answer is that there are several common patterns, and knowing which crystal contains which can tell you something about the forces you're working with.

If you feel like going deep into geology, you'll find there are a number of ways to group the different structures. If you class them as 'crystallographic point groups', there are thirty-two; if you class them as 'Bravais lattices', there are fourteen. However, the system many crystal practitioners use is crystal families. Of these there are six, so let's look at each one in turn.

**AXES IN A SHAPE** One word you'll need to know is 'axis' (with the plural being 'axes'). An axis is a line – either a real line or an imagined one – around which something can turn. The necklace string through a drilled bead, for example, works as an axis as long as it goes through the middle of the beads. Axes are the key to all crystal forms, so we'll explain them in practical terms.

Imagine a three-dimensional shape and suppose you want to pass a straight line through it so you can set it spinning evenly without wobbling – that would be an axis. You can either draw an axis from one corner through to the opposite corner (as shown here), or from the middle of a facet through to the middle of the facet opposite it.

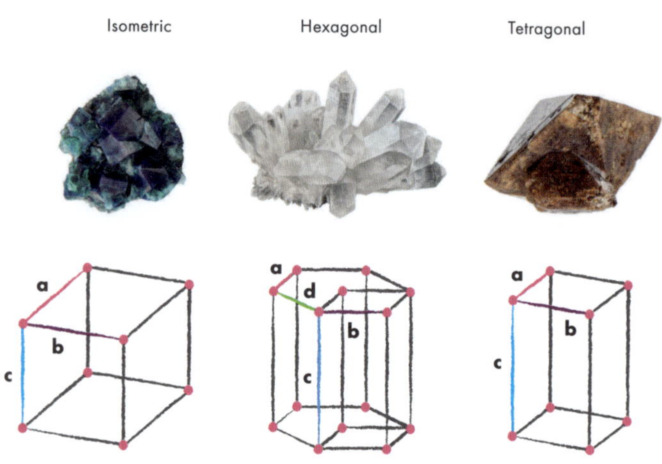

## Isometric (cubic)

Here is our dependable friend the cube: three axes at 90 degrees to each other, each the exact same length. If you need structure and grounding, this is where you can rest. Isometric crystals will help you regulate yourself, putting in order what needs to be settled and helping even you out.

## Hexagonal

Here we have four axes, forming one of the most fascinating shapes in the natural world. There's a reason bees use hexagons for their honeycombs, and it's not just because there's an amazingly efficient way to build this six-sided pattern. It's because hexagons distribute pressure with superb efficiency, making it a tremendously strong structure.

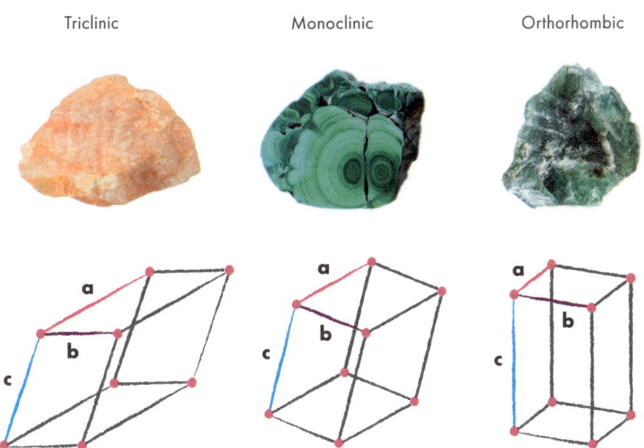

So, if you feel the need to set and explore an intention, hexagonal crystal structures are just the thing. Hexagonals will let you amplify yourself; they're associated with 'seeker' energy that will let you spread out from a secure place, powering yourself forward.

There are two varieties of this structure: some come out visibly hexagonal and some as 'triagonal/rhombohedral', meaning they have a pyramid-like three-sided appearance. As the underlying structure is the same, they are classed together here.

## Tetragonal

Once again there are three axes, but this time they are set at right angles with two of the same length and the third longer. Essentially, we're looking at a rectangle, a sturdy but dynamic form.

Tetragonal crystals are particularly attractive to thoughtful, introspective people, and can be a helpful booster when it comes to manifesting your ideas into action. They give a sense of stability and balance, helping you resolve difficulties into clear positive outcomes.

## Triclinic

These are what you might call irregular shapes, though they certainly arrange themselves into a regular lattice just like every other kind of crystal. Each molecule has three axes, but none are the same length and they branch off at three different angles, with none of them being 90 degrees.

This is a crafty structure, with its energy being adaptable and creative. If you're feeling troubled by negative energies, crystals from this family can be just the thing: like an alert guard, they're hard to fool.

By the same token they can help open you up to flexible thinking. Just as triclinic lattices create beauty out of the union of dissimilar lengths and angles, it is their energy that can speak to you if you're trying to find a way to reconcile things that seem incompatible, find a new solution or balance things that feel in tension.

At the most spiritual level, triclinic crystals are popular for astral work. What better way to get free from mundane ways of thinking than to work with a crystal that manages to make beauty out of the irregular?

## Monoclinic

Like the triclinics, monoclinics have three axes of three different lengths, but two of them meet at a right angle. Though they are not a perfectly symmetrical shape, they are a little more tidy than the triclinics.

Monoclinic structures are protectors. They purify our energy and stiffen our backbone, helping us make decisions from a stable and certain place. If you're having trouble making up your mind and need some decisiveness in your energy, a monoclinic crystal might be the one to bring into your meditations.

## Orthorhombic

Orthorhombic crystals also have three axes, each of a different length, but all of them intersecting at right angles. There's a laser-focused energy to orthorhombics: these crystals form a diamond pattern, and are powerful at 'cutting through' muddles and doubts. Since they are about dispelling negativity as well as confusion, they can be a potent emotional stone too, helping you see into the heart of a situation with greater empathy and compassion.

# Vibrations & Healing

*What do we mean when we say* that crystals can heal us through their vibrations? The answers can be subtle and complex, but one thing is for sure: many people will tell you they've been helped.

The universe – crystals, us and everything in between – is made up of energy. As we discussed when talking about atoms (see pages 10–11), electricity and motion is basically what we *are*. In particular, our bodies convey information along our nervous system, a branching interconnected superhighway that tells us what we touch, see and sense by carrying electrical charges back to our brain. In a very real sense, electricity is the language in which we think and feel.

## Good vibrations

This insight into how we connect with electricity is both new and old. The ancient Egyptians and Romans used to shock themselves with electric torpedo fish, and even the venerable Hippocrates, the 'Father of Medicine', prescribed this method as a treatment for pain. And we haven't stopped doing this: have you ever been recommended a TENS machine? The abbreviation is from 'transcutaneous electrical nerve stimulation', and this small, battery-powered device can be used during childbirth, for arthritis and other injuries. How does it work? It acts as an anaesthetic by creating a different vibration. Attach electrodes to your body, and the machine delivers a regular rhythm of safe low-voltage shocks, creating a tingling sensation that interrupts the pain signals being sent to your brain.

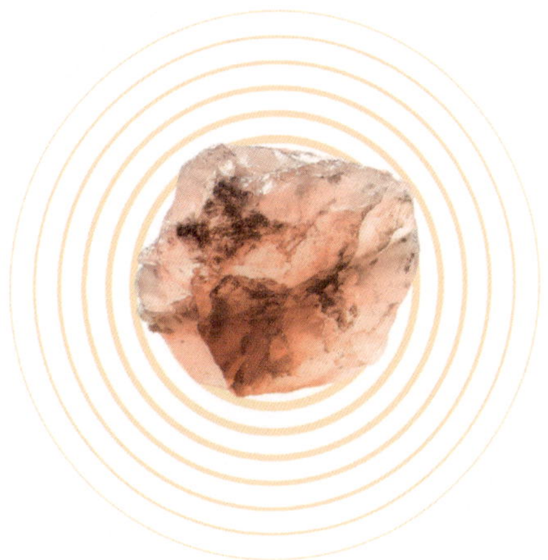

Can crystals do this for us? Well, they certainly have the power to affect electrical charges, which is why quartz is used in watches. When you place a small quartz crystal under pressure it emits a small electrical charge, which is the piezoelectric effect. It can work in reverse: if you pass a small charge through quartz, it will vibrate at predictable intervals.

---

**THE POWER OF HEAT There is also something known as the pyroelectric effect, where certain gems can emit electricity when they're heated or cooled – and fascinatingly, so can our own bones and tendons. This power in crystals was noted as far back as 314 BCE by the Greek philosopher and naturalist Theophrastus (*c.*372–*c.*287 BCE), who observed it in tourmaline, and was studied in detail from the 19th century by scientists including Pierre Curie (1859–1906), husband of Marie.**

---

## Everchanging atoms

Discoveries are still being made. As recently as 2020, researchers at the University of Warwick in England found that you can change the electric capabilities of crystals simply by putting them in contact with noble metals – which includes the gold and silver often used in jewellery. We keep finding out more about the amazing properties of these little stones, and there's more still to learn.

So, when people talk about 'cleansing' or 'charging' a crystal, they're not talking about an inert object. At the level of its atoms, a crystal is a responsive and dynamic thing.

## Cortisol and stress

One thing we do know is that the body's psychic and emotional state has a powerful impact on its physical health. We all know what it's like to get a pounding heart or a stomach ache when we're anxious, for example – but this also happens on a chemical level. Let's talk about the hormone cortisol.

Like everything our body makes, cortisol has its purpose, and it's helpful if we release it only when we need it. In this case, it is a stress hormone, where in the first moment of crisis we are flooded with adrenaline and norepinephrine, which get our heart pounding, our blood pumping and our attention laser-focused. That's the fight-or-flight response: we're ready to defend ourselves or flee – or, if we're about to make a speech in front of a crowd, to snap to full power and really give it our all.

A few minutes later the adrenal glands release cortisol, which supports the fight-or-flight response while keeping the body balanced. And if we escape the tiger or ace the speech and the stress passes, the cortisol level drops back down as we relax, and everything's as it should be.

The trouble is that a lot of us live with continual stress – and that means continually high cortisol levels. The body isn't designed to work with such high levels on a long-term basis, so this can produce all sorts of distempers: from chronic pain to mental health problems, unwanted weight gain to digestive issues, and heart disease to weakened immunity.

## Heal thyself

So, when we talk about cleansing our energy, we don't just mean picking up our mood – though, of course, you have every right to feel happy, and lifting your spirits is a perfectly good reason in and of itself. We are talking about getting the body back in balance with itself, re-aligning its natural flow so that it can do what it does best, which is heal itself.

You have your own energy flow and it's there to protect you. However, sometimes it can get misdirected; that's when chronic stress means our bodies act like there are real wolves at our door when in fact we're worried about less dramatic things. That's where redirecting it comes in. We all have the music of experience playing upon the vibrating strings of our own nerves – and the resonance of a crystal can be the helper you need to get things tuned just right.

As you approach crystals, listen to your body and your spirit. You may be surprised by the reaction you have to something: it's up to you to listen to that reaction. It's telling you something for a reason. Be open to finding out new things and see where it takes you; at the very least you'll get to enjoy the wonderful world of crystals and get some peace and calm from the meditations. And at the most? Well, who knows how high you may aspire? The whole cosmos awaits you; you're already a note in its vibrating symphony.

# The Chakras

*A word you'll often come across* when discussing or reading about crystal healing is 'chakra'. So, what exactly does it mean, and how can it help us?

The concept of chakras was popularized in the West by the spread of yoga and the New Age movement, but the original concept comes from India. They were first mentioned in the Vedas, the great Sanskrit religious texts written between 1200 and 900 BCE. They were originally a Hindu concept but were adopted into Buddhism as well, forming part of the tradition known as Tantra. The word *chakra* itself means 'wheel' or 'circle'.

To understand how a chakra works, picture your body as containing a natural flow of energy through its centre, like a river, beginning at the base of your abdomen and ending at the top of your head. At seven key points along that river are wheels that turn, letting the energy run through them. To run freely, they all need to be in good order – but if something jams or blocks them, the energy stops running through you as it should.

## A hierarchy of needs

The concept of chakras is an ancient one, but to modern psychology it's also rather elegant. A concept proposed by the American psychologist Abraham Maslow (1908–1970) fits it quite beautifully: the hierarchy of needs, often depicted as a pyramid.

Maslow's idea was this: in order to thrive, we need certain things – and crucially, the ones higher up the 'hierarchy' won't do us much good if the ones nearer the base aren't already met. Since we're modern people considering an ancient system, let's set them alongside each other.

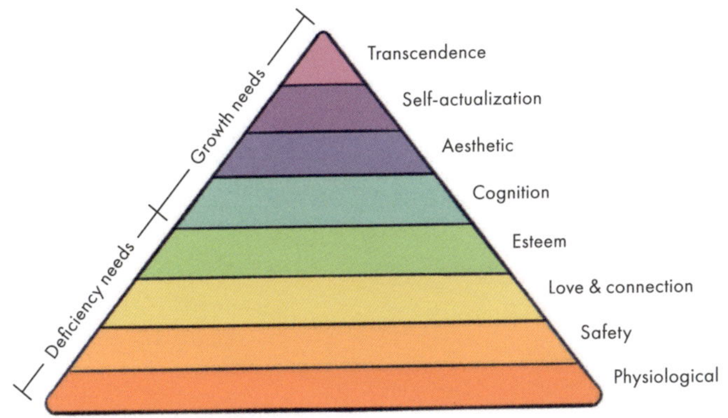


**Physiological** These are the needs of the body. They are the things we will die without: air to breathe, food and water, a reasonable temperature, shelter and adequate clothing and enough sleep. The essence of this need can be understood as 'whatever it takes to keep our physical body functioning'.

**Safety** If our physiological needs aren't met, we're in urgent danger, but there's also a degree of danger that can be measured more broadly. We need to live in a peaceful environment; we need to live around people who don't mistreat us; we need enough money to live on. We need, in short, to feel that it's basically going to be all right.

**Love and connection** This isn't just about romantic love, though of course that's a powerful motivator for many. Human beings are social animals: we need warm and compassionate contact with other people on a regular basis. Loneliness is bad for us; we need to care for other people and feel they care for us.

**Esteem** We want to think well of ourselves, and we want other people to think well of us too. Maslow considered that the esteem of others was at the lower end of this need – that prestige and respect can be very good for us as long as we don't chase them obsessively. There is a higher need to feel like a competent person who likes themselves. We also need to think well of other people – a basic respect for others makes us happier.

**Cognition** Just like your body, your brain wants exercise. Cognitive needs are about avoiding boredom, seeking out meaning, knowledge and engagement with the world. If you enjoy puzzles, analysis, mulling things over or intellectual challenges, your cognitive needs are being met.

**Aesthetic** All of us in our own way have a love of beauty. Some of us seek out poetry and fiction, music and paintings; others love a walk in the woods or a gorgeous sunset. Aesthetic needs also come out in the yearning for self-expression, whether you're an artist, a snappy dresser or a witty conversationalist.

**Self-actualization** As Maslow put it, 'What a man can be, he must be.' If we have potential, we long to use it; what is living your best life if not being the person you always aspired to be? This can be about success, social connections and aesthetic expression, but it's also about finding the healthiest way to live out your authentic personality according to your deepest values.

**Transcendence** These are the spiritual needs, the place where you reach out for the infinite. Will you ever reach it? Maybe not; maybe you'll just graze it with your fingertips – but even that is worth worlds. Transcendence is also about rising above your own personal needs, empathizing with the whole of humanity, embracing altruism and seeing the full picture.

## The different chakras

Now, let's discuss the chakras. As we talk about them nowadays, the chakras are a more synthesized system than many people realize. We associate particular colours with each, for example, but the original scriptures don't mention colours. We usually locate the third chakra around the solar plexus, but that phrase that comes from ancient Greek and Latin and wasn't talked about in those terms in the earliest texts. Likewise, Hindu traditions do not even agree about how many chakras there are! There can be as few as three chakras, as in Ayurveda, and as many as twelve in Vaishnavism. A lot of practitioners believe that there are seven main chakras, but the body has many others.

What should you take from this? Simply that, like everything else in the universe, the understanding of chakras is in a constant state of flow. It's a living tradition, and like any live thing, it changes and adapts. What we'll talk about here is the system you're most likely to encounter with crystal healing, which is graceful, helpful and a good way to understand how your own energy is moving through you. Again, we'll start at the base and work up.

Different crystals will resonate with different chakras, and you may find your own connections, but a good rule of thumb is that the colour of a crystal will speak to the colour of the chakra you want to engage.

Our needs as both physical and spiritual beings are complicated, and sometimes we will have more than one chakra that needs attention at the same time. But it can be clarifying to spend a little time meditating and directing positive energy towards the part of you that's feeling blocked. Once you open up your channels, your life force can flow more freely and your instinctive wisdom will start to speak.

## The chakras

### Root chakra

**LOCATION** Base of the spine
**COLOUR** Red
**ENERGY** Grounded; this is where you connect to the Earth, the physical world, and your basic needs as a living creature.
**NEED** I am steady and safe

---

### Sacral chakra

**LOCATION** Either below the navel or at the perineum, depending on who you talk to
**COLOUR** Orange
**ENERGY** Sensual and creative; the sacral chakra is sexuality, sensuality and play, a place where desires can be felt freely.
**NEED** I welcome pleasure

---

### Solar plexus chakra

**LOCATION** Stomach/just under the ribs
**COLOUR** Yellow
**ENERGY** Confidence and identity; here is where you hold your power and your sense of self, your ability to act and move through the world gladly.
**NEED** I value my own power

---

### Heart chakra

**LOCATION** Heart, and also the arms and hands
**COLOUR** Green
**ENERGY** Love, compassion and friendliness, both towards yourself and others; this is the place where your strength lies in your willingness to be soft.
**NEED** I embrace tenderness

---

### Throat chakra

**LOCATION** Throat and larynx (the voice box)
**COLOUR** Blue
**ENERGY** This is the chakra where truth speaks out; it's your place of self-expression, which doesn't have to be verbal if you like to communicate in other ways.
**NEED** I stand in my truth

---

### Third eye chakra

**LOCATION** Centre of the forehead
**COLOUR** Indigo/purple
**ENERGY** Insight and imagination gather here; the 'third eye' is visionary – it sees not only what's there, but also what might be visible once the mind is opened up.
**NEED** I trust my vision

---

### Crown chakra

**LOCATION** Top of the head
**COLOUR** Violet/white
**ENERGY** Transcendence; this is where we lift above ourselves and connect to the cosmos. It's the chakra of spiritual connection, to the universe, to others, and to the pure voice of our own conscience.
**NEED** I awake in the infinite

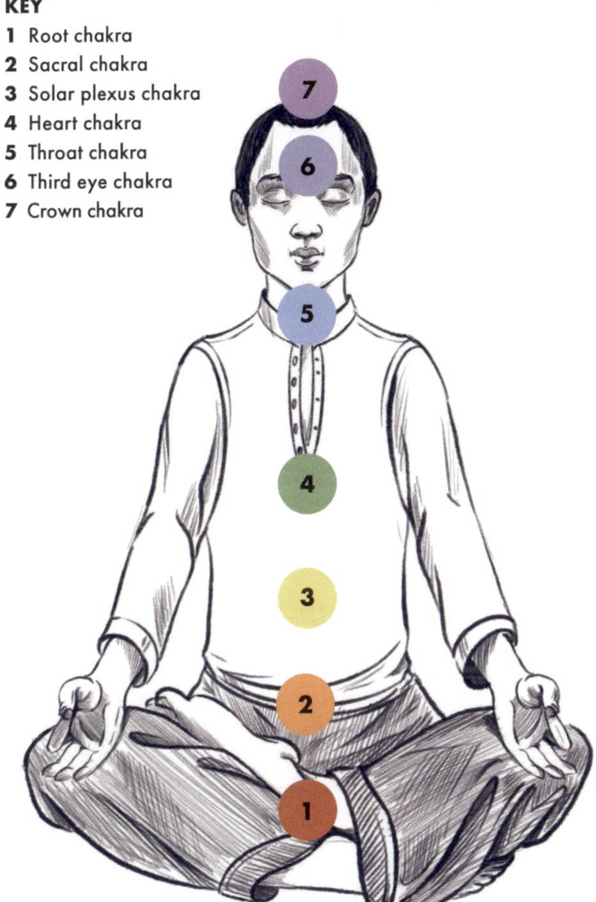
KEY
1 Root chakra
2 Sacral chakra
3 Solar plexus chakra
4 Heart chakra
5 Throat chakra
6 Third eye chakra
7 Crown chakra
7
6
5
4
3
2
1

# The Power of Colour

There's a whole field of treatment based on how colour can affect our moods, which is known as chromotherapy. (This should not be confused with light therapy, used to treat seasonal affective disorder – but that's another way in which shining energy on the body can help the spirit.) We know that too much ultraviolet light can burn the skin, but harnessing the power of gentler lights is often used to do good rather than harm.

A crystal doesn't shine a direct light on you, of course, but you wouldn't be able to see it at all if light wasn't bouncing off it, so what are the effects of different colours?

**Red** is stimulating: it boosts your energy, relieves fatigue and gets your heart moving.

**Orange** is cheering, a colour of happiness, enthusiasm and creativity.

**Yellow** brings hope and clears the mind. Like all the warm colours, it can lift the mood and stir a depressed spirit.

**Green** is the colour of balance. It can encourage health, soothe sadness and bring you to a more harmonious way of being in the world. There's some research to suggest it also helps reduce pain.

**Blue** is a colour of wakefulness (which is why sleep experts tell us to turn off our tablet a couple of hours before bed). Like all cool colours it's soothing to be around, so a blue crystal can help you relax. Blue light is used in hospitals to help babies with jaundice clear the bilirubin from their systems.

**Indigo and violet** are the colours of strength, confidence and spiritual expansion.

Let's also not forget the other colours of crystals; these come from the earth, not the sky. Browns are grounding, blacks and silvers potent and protective, golds are enriching, and whites clear and purifying.

# Crystal Shapes

*Every crystal has its own* underlying structure, but there's another aspect to consider when holding a gemstone: the shape you can see and touch.

What a crystal looks like at a microscopic level (see page 10) will be very different from the form that you will interact with by using your own senses – and that form can have just as powerful an impact. A glittering, sharp-tipped geode and a smooth egg you can rub for comfort might be the same stone geologically, but obviously your experience of them will be distinct to each one. Remember, you're bringing *yourself* to the practice as well as the crystal, and the tangible is a huge part of the process.

As with everything about crystal healing, the first step is to listen to your own energy. If a particular shape of crystal calls out to you and you can't explain why, it doesn't matter if it's not the usual shape for the need you wish it to serve. It's speaking to you for a reason, and you'll find that reason as you work within yourself. Nobody is such a simple being that one shape or resonance can answer everything about them, so let yourself be open to your own instinctive discoveries.

However, as a starting point, let's discuss some common shapes you may find and their particular implications.

## Geodes

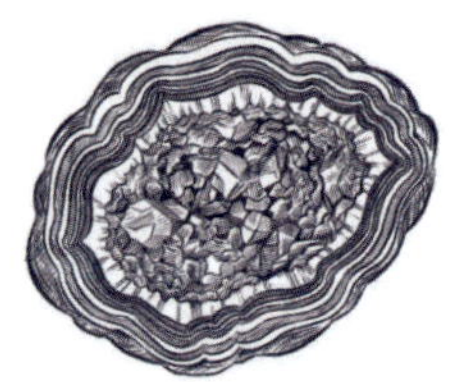

These are crystals in a natural manifestation that has an outer layer enclosing the faceted forms within. Rock hunters love finding them because it's like unwrapping a birthday present – crack open a plain-looking stone and you'll find a sparkling one inside. The commonest kind is amethyst, but other kinds of quartz such as agate and citrine can also form geodes, as can pyrite, haematite and various others.

Spiritually, there are some lovely resonances in this stone. The tips of the crystals all point inwards, a reminder that your heart and soul are at your core; if you want to do some work with your heart chakra or take some time to reflect deeply, a geode may be a good choice. There is the protective energy from the outer shell, providing a strong shield for the more delicate and subtle manifestations within. You can also channel a geode's energy to remind you of the abundance of the world, a place that can forge wonders from within itself, always holding more glorious surprises.

## Clusters

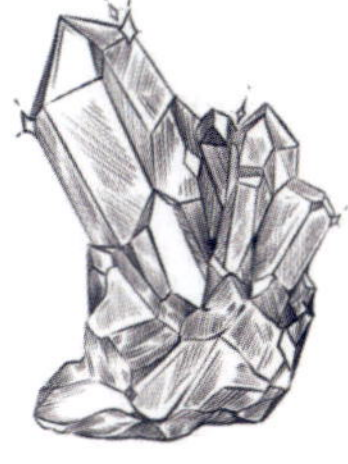

A cluster is a group of faceted crystals that have grown alongside each other. Where geodes form inside enclosed spaces, clusters need an open space. Multiple crystal structures grow together from the same base, like trees in a forest growing from the same soil that are independent but united.

Clusters have a positive, neighbourly energy that can be a marvellous amplifier. Do you feel like your whole self is a bit scattered and needs drawing together? Or do you want to create echoes that will amplify your intentions? A cluster might be just what you need: a whole that's greater than the sum of its parts.

Likewise, the harmony of the crystals growing together can be a great tool for balance and healing. The image of a cluster is an icon of reconciliation, with forms that find beauty in their side-by-side existence while retaining their independent shapes.

## Wands

Sometimes crafters polish crystals into wand shapes, and sometimes single crystals naturally form a long, narrow tower or point.

The wands are among the most subtle and complex of the crystal shapes simply because there are so many varieties: some are pointed or flat at one end, some at both; they vary in their facets, their regularity and their heft. What we can say of all of them is that they're generators and clearers of blockages.

Wands 'point', channelling the energy in your chosen direction. A flat end is stable while a faceted end is dynamic. A pyramid tip has resonances that build from a solid base to higher realms, while a smoother end is calming and pacifying.

## Eggs and worry stones

These are polished creations, deliberately carved and smoothed into shapes that will feel comforting in your hand.

The egg invokes potential and things yet 'unhatched'; it also is one of the strongest shapes nature has created because of how evenly it distributes pressure, which can be a great thing if you are feeling like your life needs more balance. If you have a stiff muscle or an aching feeling, rolling an egg over the spot can be tremendously soothing.

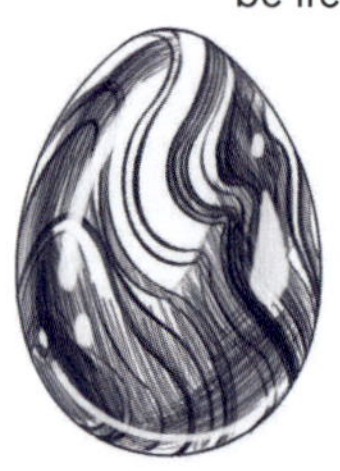

A worry stone, meanwhile, is a sturdy oval, sometimes with a dip in it for your thumb to rub, hence the other names 'thumb stone' or 'palm stone'. These are portable allies, a place to touch for steadiness and guidance when you're out and about – though remember to carry them wrapped safely as you don't want your keys to damage them!

## Gazing stones

Sometimes stones can be shaped specifically to encourage your sight – that is, to rest your eyes upon them and see what your vision suggests.

The crystal ball of legend is, of course, the most famous sort. Ball shapes are good for spreading energy evenly in all directions, and they can also be used for scrying, or gazing upon a reflective or transluscent surface and opening your subconscious mind up to messages. The mirror shape, especially in obsidian, is another form that's been used throughout history, with its flat surface polished to reflect your thoughts back at you.

## Tumbled/unshaped

Not every stone will take on a shape, either naturally or by a carver, into any particular form – and a lot of the most affordable crystals are little scraps that have either been left raw or smoothed off by being put through a tumbler.

We might consider these all-purpose crystals, and crystals of authenticity. They are what they are – and that has a power all its own.

## Decorative shapes

Many dealers sell crystals worked into particular shapes, such as hearts. These can be fun but are best approached on an individual basis. Do they speak to you, reflect your intentions and feel good in your hand, or do they feel like someone else's design? Crystals set into jewellery also fall into this category.

# Birthstones

*Are you looking for a stone* that goes particularly well with your date of birth? If you are, the good news is that you may have a bit of choice, but the bad news is that not everyone agrees about which stone works best for which month!

However, certain crystals are generally agreed upon, and that each month tends towards a particular energy. What folllows is the most broadly accepted birthstone choices, with the reminder that if your particular birthstone doesn't seem to do much for you, there's often a multiple choice – and even if there isn't, you don't have to work with a crystal that isn't helping you. Birthstones should be taken as suggestions rather than mandates; they might have some particular benefits, but the best judge of that is you.

## January: garnet

This is one of the most agreed-upon birthstones. Garnets are popular with jewellers because they're hard and resilient; while they're usually thought of as red, they can come in a variety of colours ranging from pink to brown to green to black. If a red garnet doesn't appeal to you, you still have quite a bit of choice. It's a stone of love, meditation and revival.

## February: amethyst

Here's another birthstone most practitioners agree upon. One of the most beautiful and beloved varieties of quartz, amethyst comes in shades of purple and can be found in faceted crystals and geodes as well as polished stones. Amethyst is a balancer and an amplifier, especially of intuition; it's a crystal that can bring you good energy in almost any situation.

## March: aquamarine, blue topaz and bloodstone

Aquamarine is green-blue, a stone of courage and calming. Blue topaz, like all topazes, is a clarifier, especially for self-reflection and affirmation. Bloodstone is mottled in shades of red and green – the blood of the body and the life of the leaves, we could say; it's a healer, teacher and grounder. What these all have in common is that they speak to us to find truth from a quiet place, and then turn it outwards with all the strength we have gathered there.

## April: diamond or 'crystal'

When people say 'crystal' in this context they generally mean any clear, faceted stone that bears a resemblance to diamond. The likeliest reason for this is that diamonds themselves are both expensive and often tied to unethical trading, hence the term 'blood diamond', so they may not be for everybody. What we should perhaps take from this is that you need a stone with the *energy* of a diamond rather than being one exactly – this might be a lab-grown diamond (see page 82), or it could be a purifier and amplifier like clear quartz.

**January**
**GARNET**

**February**
**AMETHYST**

**March**
**AQUAMARINE**

**May**
**EMERALD**

**June**
**MOONSTONE**

## May: emerald or chrysoprase

Emeralds can be clear or cloudy green, while the more affordable chrysoprase is opaque green or lemon-yellow. Both are stones of hope, inspiration and the joy of living, and they can connect to the heart chakra to uplift you into embracing your present and your future.

## June: pearl, moonstone or alexandrite

Of course, pearls aren't stones (so they aren't included in the directory) – but what do they share with the luminous moonstone and alexandrite, the 'emerald by day, ruby by night' stone that changes colour according to the light? These are all shimmerers, iridescent and fluid, and are responsive to their surroundings.

## July: ruby or carnelian

Both have a warm, accepting and vigorous energy: they're physical and potent with plenty of strength. Carnelian, a grounding and cleansing stone, is a good budget option.

## August: peridot, spinel, sardonyx or green amethyst

Sardonyx tends towards dark shades and is a stone of stability, while spinel has many colours and is a renewer. Peridot is a gem-like cleanser that lifts burdens and helps you let go of negativity. Green amethyst, meanwhile, is a bit of a magic trick: in its natural form it's extremely rare, but a version called 'prasiolite' can be created by heat-treating regular purple amethyst. If we're seeing a common theme here, it's transformation: if you can steady yourself, you'll be ready to rise up refreshed and inspired.

## September: sapphire or lapis lazuli

Both are beautiful blues (though sapphire can also come in many other colours), which connects them to the throat chakra, the site of clarity and truth. These are stones of wisdom and enlightenment.

## October: opal, tourmaline and rose quartz

Technically, opals aren't crystals – they don't have that lattice structure. Regardless, what they are is magically beautiful, with a shifting iridescence that fascinates. Tourmaline, meanwhile, can come in a wide range of lovely hues, often within the same stone. The shades within rose quartz can be more subtle, but they come from the same place: a vibration where your energy

**July**
**RUBY**

**August**
**PERIDOT**

**September**
**LAPIS LAZULI**

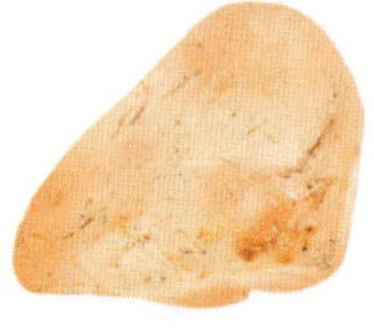

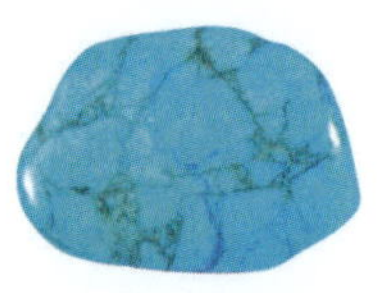

**October**
**OPAL**

**November**
**TOPAZ**

**December**
**TURQUOISE**

is embraced in all its manifestations. These stones are rainbows, subtle and ever-changing, and within that is the freedom to be your true self.

## November: topaz, citrine and smoky quartz

Topaz is a communicative stone, shifting through a wide range of shades to help you express every aspect of yourself. Citrine is a sunny, positive stone that will help you build your self-esteem for new beginnings. Smoky quartz has a strong root chakra energy, helping you shift negative to positive and face challenges steady on your feet. Put these together, and their energy will guide you towards self-acceptance as you prepare to move on: by embracing your natural identity, you will have the strength to start out for better things.

## December: turquoise and zircon

Turquoise is often considered lucky; it can deflect bad forces and create an energized, harmonious state of mind, so you can aspire high. Zircon inspires connections to the divine, which can fire you up with enthusiasm and help to draw out your virtuous qualities. These will bring out your best self: if you're feeling ambitious, meditation with these can help you approach your goals with passion and go about it in the healthiest of ways.

## Other options

If one or more of these stones speaks to you but it doesn't happen to be your personal birthstone, does that mean it won't respond to your energy the same way? Not at all. It just points to some different paths.

You can, for instance, meditate on the birthstone of a month that isn't 'your' birthstone. If you were born in June but you want a prosperous February, say, meditating on amethyst during February could be one way to help you focus on the particular needs and strengths associated with that energy. All of these good vibes can benefit us, and sometimes setting aside a month to pay special attention to one set in particular could be a way to keep yourself spiritually well rounded.

Finally, if you encounter a practitioner who has their own ideas about birthstones, don't assume they're 'wrong'. Listen to what they have to say; if they're a perceptive person, they might very well have some new and interesting things to teach you.

# Sourcing Crystals

*How should you go about* shopping for crystals? There's no single correct answer, only the choice that's right for you – but here are some of the commonest options.

Before you begin, a word about ethical sourcing. Crystals are usually obtained by mining, and that can have negative impacts both on the environment and, if the labour conditions are bad, on the people doing the mining and polishing. A seller will have their own chain of supply and some are more careful about these things than others, so you can learn a lot by asking them how ethically their crystals are sourced. We serve our own spirits by respecting our consciences, our planet and our fellow people.

## Specialist shops

Consider looking for a crystal in one of the small, independent shops that places crystal expertise front and centre. The main drawback is that not everyone lives within reach of a good one, but if you do, it can be a great place to look for something new.

As well as supporting a local business, you should be able to handle the crystals and see how each one feels in response to your own energy – assuming the shopkeeper doesn't mind. There should be an opportunity to chat to the owner or staff, who can tell you directly about their sourcing, and it's very likely they have a lot of knowledge about crystals, as well as possible connections in the neighbourhood crystal community.

## Craft fairs

A lot of crystal enthusiasts sell by setting up a temporary stall at local craft events, farmers' markets and even pop-ups in main shopping areas. It makes perfect sense: for many people this is a passionate hobby rather than a full-time trade, so this is a way for them to sell and meet people on a scale they can afford. Like shopkeepers, they can be great to chat to; they're usually doing it for love of crystals, after all.

## Gem and mineral shows

You'll find all sorts of people here, not just those interested in crystal healing but also geology and jewellery-making. Which is all good! As long as everyone respects the others' beliefs, a diverse range will just enrich the energy of the show – and you'll certainly get the chance to check out a lot of options.

## Museum gift shops

Museums that have a scientific or natural history bent often sell a few crystals as part of their stock. It may be harder to get information about ethical sourcing as it's not their speciality, but there's no harm in trying.

## Online

Of course, you won't be able to handle the crystals before you buy, but on the other hand you will have access to a much wider choice – and if you know what you're looking for or are particularly struck by a picture of something, you're headed in the right direction. Contact forms or email should be there to ask sourcing questions.

Another advantage of online shopping is that you can compare prices without causing any offence. This is a good way to get a good sense of what's a fair price. You can even do this without making a purchase and then take that knowledge with you when you go to shop somewhere else.

# Crystal Care

*Before using a new crystal,* you'll want to cleanse it and set your intentions, and if you care for your crystal with the respect it deserves, it will take care of you for a lifetime.

## Cleansing a crystal

Once you bring a new crystal into your home, the first thing you will want to do is cleanse it. This process can remove any energies, negative or otherwise, that the crystal may have absorbed from the people who handled it before you and from the environment it was in. There are several ways to cleanse a crystal, though not all of them are recommended. You may come across advice to wash or submerge a new crystal in salt, but salt is corrosive to anything, especially if it gets into tiny nooks and crannies, and a sudden temperature change can cause cracks. Besides this, there are crystals such as lapis lazuli, topaz, moonstone and malachite that are actively damaged by water. The following gentler methods are recommended.

**Bathe it in moonlight** Place your crystal where it will be exposed to moonlight for a few hours. Some people advise setting them in sunlight, but certain crystals such as amethyst can fade, so the gentler moonlight is a better choice. However, don't leave the crystal outside (you never know what can happen). Setting it on a windowsill is fine.

**Place it with cleansing crystals** Selenite and clear quartz are popular choices for cleansing the energy in other crystals. Just make sure to keep them apart to avoid scratches.

**Burn, or smudge, sage** Light a bundle of sage; after a few seconds blow out the flame and then pass it over the crystal. The smoke will banish negative influences. Palo santo and other sacred herbs can also be used.

**Sound** Many people use cleansing vibrations from a sound bowl or tingshas (small cymbals).

**A purifying meditation** This involves setting aside some time to fill the crystal up with your own visualization: surround it with healing light and clean energy.

## Setting your intention

Once the crystal is cleansed, you can programme it by setting your intention. In this way you can let your crystal get to know you and what you would like it to help you with. In a calm place hold the crystal in your hands or against the chakra you most want to work on and picture your energy flowing into it with your thoughts and the question you wish to have help with.

## Regular care

Clean your crystals regularly, such as when it's a new month, a new lunar phase or when you wish to set a new intention.

To avoid scratches, place your crystals on a smooth surface, dust them with non-abrasive cloths, and ensure you only keep smooth, polished or tumbled stones together in a bag.

Be mindful of fading: strong direct sunlight is more of a problem for some crystals than others, but it's never sensible to leave them in the full blast of sunlight long-term.

# Meditation

*There are many different styles* of meditation. Here are two which are nice and simple and can help to give you a start in meditation with crystals.

Always cleanse your crystal before meditating (see pages 40–41); if you plan to use it regularly, you could use sage or send purifying energy rather than anything more hands-on. This will also help prepare your own spirit for calm and acceptance.

## Exploratory meditation

This is a good practice to try with a crystal that speaks to the heart or the throat chakras. Do you have a question you're trying to answer for yourself? Do you feel out of sorts but aren't sure why? Or do you just want to spend some time in self-reflection? This meditation is a good choice.

After cleansing your crystal, sit comfortably so that you're upright and alert but not stiff. Place your crystal in front of you where you can easily rest your gaze upon it. Look at it steadily and hold your intention in your mind: silently ask it the question.

Now let the question go. Trust the crystal's potency and your own sensitivity to it, and let your conscious mind stop chasing for answers. As your eyes stay on the crystal, settle your attention into your breathing. Focus on your exhale, picturing your stress and negativity leaving your body along with the air. Then move your focus to your inhale, enjoying the energizing sensation as your body draws in the nourishing oxygen. Once you feel ready, move your attention to the sensation of your breathing as a complete process, a perfect circle of intake and release. Let your whole body become present to you.

As you do this, keep the crystal in your sight and listen to the energies flowing through you. If random thoughts pass through your mind, just let them drift past like bubbles along a stream and they'll flow away. But pay attention, too, to the answers your mind and body are giving you. Are you feeling extra tension in a chakra, or in places in your flesh that hold tension or trauma? Do certain emotions keep resurfacing?

It's okay if you don't get a complete answer and perfect solution in a single session! Just stay open and hear what the energies are telling you, and your insight will come over time.

## Empowerment meditation

Are you facing a challenge? Feeling rather down on yourself? Recovering from a bad time? We all need a bit of a boost sometimes, so choose a crystal with good connections to the root or solar plexus chakra. You can also do this with a personal favourite crystal that vibrates in harmony with you.

After cleansing your crystal, set it where you can gaze on it, and sit comfortably. Relax your body and mind, letting distractions come and go.

Now fill yourself with your intention. This can be a single word, such as 'courage' or 'healing'. Or you might prefer an affirmation. Avoid negative phrasing; rather than saying 'I'm not worried', you could say 'I face life with confidence' or 'I am calm and steady.' Fill yourself with this intention, learning the energy of the place where it is true.

After each meditation, spending a few moments of quiet with a grounding crystal can help you transition back to regular life.

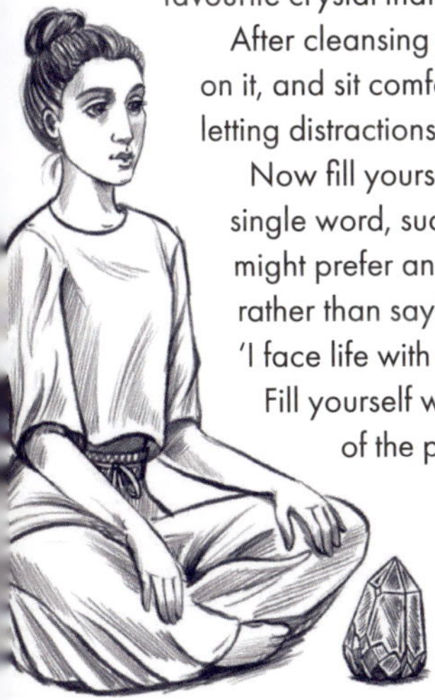

# Agate

**COLOUR** many shades, sometimes including dyed

**PATTERNING** banded, often with a ripple effect

**INTERNAL STRUCTURE** hexagonal/monoclinic

**ORIGIN** worldwide

*Crystals can be like a living species:* closely related to each other at cellular level, but so different in how they turn out that in practice they are talked about as different beings. There are few stones that manifest this quality as dramatically as agate.

Technically, agate is a variant of chalcedony (see page 74), which is responsible for its complex structural lattice. However, it would be far too reductive to talk about these crystals as if they are all the same: agate is a gloriously various stone that bursts with colour and abundance. The common factor is that it has a beautiful 'banded' appearance, its crystals forming in layers that mark it like the surface of a lake where a bird has landed, with ripples spreading in a pattern of response and dynamism.

We'll talk about the particular qualities of popular varieties of agate, but regardless what they all have in common is agate being a steadying stone. It grounds you, helping to clear your mind and balance your emotions, which can clear your energy to put strength behind your intentions.

## Agate variants

**Blue lace agate** is an elegant crystal, with its delicate shades of sky blue and star white linking it to the throat and crown chakras and bringing you to a state where you can speak your truth from a place of connection to the whole of the cosmos or humanity. As you meditate on its radiating bands, picture them washing away your confusion so only clarity and gentleness radiate out from you.

**Crazy lace agate** is any variant that contains the banding in a complex, swirling pattern; it is good for a sense of playfulness, experimentation and freedom from constraint.

**Dendritic agate** is any agate that contains an array of minerals spreading out in a fern-like pattern that invokes the feeling of slow and ancient growth. These 'dendrites' are often of manganese ore, which invokes bonding and empowers us to work with others. Dendritic agate is associated with plenitude.

**Fire agate**, like the flame it invokes, can glow in shades of red and orange, as well as the green and blue of fiercer heats. It is linked to the root chakra, the force and vitality of our primal selves. It is also a stone of cleansing, a fire that burns away impurities; because of this, many practitioners think of it as a crystal of perfection. Nobody's actually perfect, of course, and it can hurt us to ask it of ourselves, but if you're engaged in a goal that calls for discipline and refinement, then fire agate can be a vigorous ally. If there are little imperfections in your particular piece, use them to remind yourself that 'perfect' doesn't have to mean 'flawless': the fire will burn in the heart regardless of any imperfections.

**Fortification agate** is a common and popular variant: its banded patterning makes up a set of concentric shapes that may or may not have a cavity at their centre. It's an arrangement that invokes the fortifications of a castle, layer upon layer of protective walls that guard the cherished residents within. The outside world can put pressure on us, so fortification agate is a good energy to invoke when you need to put up your own boundaries – either standing your ground against people besieging you or shoring up your spirit against worries attacking you from within. The bands are often tinted with different metals – iron, manganese, chromium, titanium – reminding us of all the resources we have within ourselves and the world.

**Moss agate** has a charming variegation: fine strands of green and earth tones growing in a filigree shape, evocative of moss and lichen patterns in nature. As such it's a stone of connection to growth, abundance and renewal. It is also a crystal of appreciation of the living world, with healing qualities and power to refresh the spirit.

# Alexandrite

**COLOUR** 'emerald by day, ruby by night'

**PATTERNING** transluscent to transparent, clear or with delicate striations

**INTERNAL STRUCTURE** orthorhombic

**ORIGIN** first discovered in the Russia's Ural Mountains; also mined in Brazil, India, Madagascar, Myanmar, Sri Lanka, Tanzania and Zimbabwe

*Alexandrite – a variant of chrysoberyl* – has a special property: it changes colour depending on its environment. Under daylight or fluorescent light, it shows a warm green tone, but under incandescent light it turns a rich red.

This magic trick makes alexandrite one of the most prized and expensive of crystals, and it's greatly valued by jewellers. Along with moonstone, it's a birthstone for June.

## Forgiveness and balance

Happily, all forms of chrysoberyl – including common variants in a more affordable price range – are stones of spiritual generosity, which is what Latin-speaking Christians called *caritas* and Buddhists call *metta*. Their power is in forgiveness, helping us to take a gentle attitude towards both ourselves and others, recognizing human value and the tenderness it deserves. Because of this, chrysoberyl is a stone of great spiritual strength, helping us explore the world with creativity and openness as it helps us to stop anger and bitterness holding us back.

Alexandrite adds a twist to this: its changeability is good for when you're trying to strike a balance between the external and internal world, the physical and the spiritual. Transformation and the reconciliation of its opposites is in its very nature.

If you're feeling wobbly, alexandrite may not be the best choice: you should begin with something more grounding so that you can get your feet on the ground first, or else pair it with a stabilizing stone in your meditation and invoke both of them together. If you do feel uncertain, though, return to the central energy of chrysoberyl, which is the power of compassion for both self and others – you can never go too far wrong when that's the foundation you stand upon.

# Amber

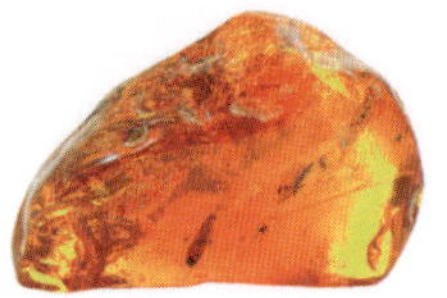

**COLOUR** orange

**PATTERNING** clear, sometimes with cracked flaws and pieces of suspended organic matter

**INTERNAL STRUCTURE** organic

**ORIGIN** Baltic amber comes from the Baltic region, especially the Kalingrad Oblast of Russia

*Amber isn't a crystal, or even a stone:* it's a form of fossilised tree sap from conifers that grew in the Eocene, a geological epoch that took place between 59 and 33.9 million years ago. Scientists aren't in complete agreement about which tree or trees exactly produced that resin, and varieties of amber have been found in Northern Europe, the Mediterranean, Middle East, Asia and North Africa. Regardless, the amber you're most likely to access, especially if it's jewellery grade, is Baltic, from Sambia, also known as the Zemlandic or Kalingrad Peninusla.

Despite all this, amber has all the social and spiritual resonance of a crystal: it's been used both in jewellery and folk healing as long as true crystals.

## Nuturing nature

Because of its organic origin, amber is a healing stone with the power of the sun in its heart. Like sunshine, it radiates nourishment, nurturing and cleansing that will help us to be free to unfurl. This is a gem that has travelled through time to reach you, from the lifeblood of a tree to a glowing creation you can hold in your hand. Amber's power is transformative, but it's a slow transformation of healthy growth rather than one that is quick as a flash, allowing us to develop our energies at a steady pace. Our vitality will thrive because it comes from a place of balance.

In essence, amber is a gem that absorbs negative energy. It has endured time and pressure and come out strong and glowing. Think of this, and it can be a safe place to put your own stresses when you need to refine them.

# Amethyst

**COLOUR** purple

**PATTERNING** varies from transluscent to opaque – in raw a state, clusters in crystal geodes; polished, shades from deep purple to pale lavender and almost white

**INTERNAL STRUCTURE** hexagonal

**ORIGIN** mostly mined in Russia until the 19th century; now frequently mined in Brazil, as well as across Africa, Asia, Europe and the Americas

*Amethyst is a crystal beloved across history* for its beautiful rich colouring and its power to create peace. It is one of the most famous in all of crystal healing as well as a semi-precious stone of choice for jewellers; this make it easy to get your hands on, and you'll have a wide of forms and shapes to choose from.

Scientifically, amethyst is a variant of quartz – quite a lot of the most popular crystals are – but it's so special and widely admired that it definitely deserves its own category. It's often recommended for beginners due to it having a natural spirituality and its appeal for aiding a contented and balanced state of mind. If you're new to meditation, it's a great place to start.

Its purple shade connects it to the crown chakra, a site for opening higher states of consciousness and connecting with the infinite. It is a particularly spiritual stone, very good for meditation.

The colour purple has a long cultural connection to prosperity and splendour – it was the choice of emperors in times past – so if you're feeling the need for more abundance in your life, amethyst is a good ally.

## For purity and cleansing

In everyday life amethyst has a particular power to transmute, purify and make things clean. If there's bad energy around you or swirling within your feelings, this is a crystal that can convert that negativity into love and healing. Amethyst protects, not by bouncing negativity away but by transfiguring it into something more positive.

This is a crystal you can use to 'clean house' mentally and spiritually: if you've got a difficult decision to take or a painful emotion you're grappling with, amethyst energy can help you get back to your centre. From there you can accept things for how they are and make the best choices on where to go from here. Use its powers to slow down your chattering thoughts and allow yourself to relax into clear thinking, choosing your path forward from a tranquil place.

The simplifying power of amethyst is also great if you're experiencing insomnia. A polished crystal under your pillow or near your resting head may be just the thing to ease you into a more tranquil night with dreams that bring you the insight you're searching for. (Be aware that amethyst fades in sunlight, so never keep it right by a window.)

## Green amethyst

A variant worth mentioning is 'green amethyst', which is one of the birthstones for August. There are two ways you can acquire one, so let's clear up any confusion: there is naturally occurring green amethyst, which is rare and consequently expensive. There is also prasiolite, which is what you get when you put regular purple amethyst through a process of heat treatment, or, if you want a particularly pale shade, irradiation – though

the latter is not so stable and, if exposed to temperatures above 150 degrees Celsius, it can fade until colourless. Different countries have rules about whether you can call prasiolite 'green amethyst', and some people may use the terms interchangeably or just mix them up.

Does a heat treatment process make the stone less powerful? Not necessarily; after all, the Earth heat-treated magma to make crystals in the first place. Whereas the purple will speak to the crown, the green shade will speak to the heart chakra, and you can see it as a way to bring your emotions into communication with your spirit – which, in people as in crystals, sometimes takes a little extra help. Be guided by your own instincts when it comes to green amethyst or prasiolite; you will know best what speaks to you.

---

**Whether a green amethyst or another variant, be careful of exposing it to too much sunlight to avoid fading.**

---

# Ametrine

**COLOUR** yellow and purple

**PATTERNING** transparent, but can be cloudy in less expensive forms

**INTERNAL STRUCTURE** hexagonal

**ORIGIN** Bolivia

*Ametrine is something rather wonderful:* a combination of amethyst and citrine, two of the most popular crystals among practitioners. Almost all naturally occur ametrine comes from a single mine in Bolivia, but the more affordable kind may be heat-treated amethyst that in its original form was entirely purple. How you feel about that is up to you, but physically it's just the same as the natural variety: both citrine and amethyst are variants of quartz, and the fact that they both occur in ametrine happens because the Earth itself created them under conditions of uneven temperature.

## Strength and wisdom

Ametrine can balance the benefits of each of its composite crystals. Citrine is sunny and regenerative, while amethyst is harmonious and spiritual, transfiguring bad energy into good. Taken together, this is a powerful combination: your solar plexus chakra will be energized by the citrine, stimulating your personal power, while the amethyst will help to open your third eye chakra, a site of vision and imaginative insight.

Ametrine is a crystal to turn to when you want to balance your inner and outer powers. You will be connecting the aspects of your own spirit and personality in a harmonious blend, both charging yourself up and appreciating the value of reconciliation. From here you can approach the world knowing not only that you can act, but you can act wisely.

---

**You can achieve similar benefits to ametrine by doing a double meditation with a piece of amethyst along with a piece of citrine, beginning with a visualization that creates a flow of energy between the two of them.**

---

# Apatite

**COLOUR** usually blue or blue-green, but can also be colourless or shades of pink and purple to yellow or brown

**PATTERNING** transparent or translucent, sometimes with a marbling effect

**INTERNAL STRUCTURE** hexagonal

**ORIGIN** Brazil, Mexico and Myanmar are major sources for jeweller quality, but Asia, Africa and the Americas also have deposits

*This is a crystal that jewellers prize,* so it can be one of the pricier ones, with clearer stones being more expensive. The good news is that for a spiritual practice you don't need the fancy stuff: the energy is clarifying even if the crystal isn't a high-grade one, especially when you combine it with your own intentions.

Because apatite comes in a range of colours, different stones may speak more to different chakras. All, though, have a connection to the throat chakra, and because it's a crystal of clear seeing, apatite will call for you to be in a place of truth, to allow your judgement and instincts find what they know to be right.

## Connecting to dreams

If you're feeling mentally cloudy, apatite is an excellent crystal for stimulating your intellect and getting you to sharpen up. It may respond more to your rational side – perhaps you have a problem you need to think through or a puzzle you'd like to resolve – but it can also manifest in the form of spiritual insight or creative inspiration. Apatite gets your mind moving.

This makes it a good choice if you're engaged in any sort of visionary search. A good method is to place apatite near where you sleep and allow your energies to reach out to connect with the crystal and reach a place of wise dreaming – either lucid moments where you can make choices, or your mind sorting through what it knows so your dreams can give you back your own knowledge in a clearer form.

---

**Apatite is relatively soft and brittle and shouldn't be knocked about, so don't slip it under your pillow and hope for the best: make sure it's properly secured and protected.**

---

# Aquamarine

**COLOUR** blue-green

**PATTERNING** transparent/translucent

**INTERNAL STRUCTURE** hexagonal

**ORIGIN** Brazil, Pakistan, Madagascar, Mozambique, Nigeria and Zambia

*Aquamarine is a variety of beryl* and, being popular with jewellers, it can be expensive. It's also a birthstone for the month of March.

The delicate colouring – somewhere between blue and green – makes this a stone that speaks to both the heart and throat chakras, calling for you to speak your truth from a place that both loves and accepts the need to love others. It's also a hue much associated with water, and the sea in particular, so if that's an element that has particular spiritual significance for you, then aquamarine can be a great energy to get yourself back in the flow of things.

## Calm, courage and sensitivity

Above all, aquamarine is a stone of courage, though not a stone of confrontation; its energy is cooling, not hot-headed. It allows us to think things through steadily and approach our problems well-prepared – both intellectually and emotionally. By coming at things with both truth and compassion, we allow for the fact that yes, sometimes we're scared, and sometimes we can be too quick to jump to judgements about other people – usually because fear is making us hypervigilant. Aquamarine helps that anxiety to melt away, flowing back into the ocean of the universe and leaving us calm.

People can sometimes associate sensitivity with cowardice, but the lesson of aquamarine is the opposite. Acting on impulse without self-knowledge can lead to regret, while sensitivity can be the beginnings of understanding, and understanding the beginnings of real strength. If you're someone who has a lot of feelings, aquamarine may be a stone that you feel a kinship with. Its qualities will allow us to be expressive, whether it's being honest with ourself or communicating with others.

# Aventurine

**COLOUR** usually green, but also shades of blue, yellow, orange, red or white

**PATTERNING** transluscent and shimmering

**INTERNAL STRUCTURE** hexagonal

**ORIGIN** Primarily India (sometimes called 'Indian Jade'); also Brazil, China and Russia

*Aventurine has a delightful quality* that contributes to its auspicious vibrations: it shimmers. It shimmers so distinctively, in fact, that geologists call this quality is 'aventurescence'. The reason is due to its mineral inclusions – minute plates of minerals trapped in the early stages of the crystal's formation and becoming a part of the whole that glitters bright little spangles that catch the light. It's a thoroughly cheering sight.

This positive energy is what aventurine can bring to meditation. It doesn't encourage you to be bossy or bullying with others; on the contrary, it promotes a kindly and loving attitude – but it also helps you to know what you want and need, and to feel strong enough to say so, perhaps even helping guide others along the way. It connects to the heart chakra and brings with it a sense of emotional abundance: meditating with aventurine can help you love and celebrate yourself, recognizing your value and appreciating what you have to contribute.

## Bringing opportunity

Aventurine is known as the 'stone of opportunity': it's a stone of leadership, prosperity and good fortune. If your life isn't thriving as you'd like, this is the energy you might need.

This is a crystal to consider if you're thinking about taking a chance. Of course, there is no guarantee that an aventurine stone in your pocket will help you beat a casino – don't do anything silly! However, if you've decided that you want to make a creative leap, aventurine can help you power up the confidence to jump with a joyful energy to help you over the hurdles. It's a stone of opportunity, not because it can conjure the opportunities up, but because it puts you in a mental space to spot and create them for yourself.

# Beryl

**COLOUR** many variants, including blue, pink, green, yellow and white

**PATTERNING** clear in its pure form, but often opaque from impurities

**INTERNAL STRUCTURE** hexagonal

**ORIGIN** Brazil, Madagascar, Columbia, China, United States, sub-Saharan Africa and South Asia

*Beryl can take many forms*, and some of these are famous in their own right: emerald and aquamarine are part of the beryl family, as is a pink variant known as morganite, and bixbite, or red beryl, which is quite rare. What they all have in common is that this is a stone of healing.

Because there are so many ways life can knock us about, it's fortunate that beryl comes in so many colours. You may like to choose a piece whose colour links it particularly to the chakra you feel has been most overloaded by troubles: pink can bring a sense of gentleness and love, while blue can open your throat chakra if you're worn down by being unable to say what was on your mind. Let your instincts guide you here: there's no bad choice, and the healing energy can always work through us.

## Letting go of the past

The energy of beryl can lift us out of our stress. Life can get on top of us sometimes, but if you're stuck in that state of mind, then it's bad for you physically, mentally and spiritually: to get better we need to let go of the baggage that's weighing us down.

A meditation with beryl is calming, and it's also good for creating a sense of clarity and confidence. Past traumas can clutter the mind, and when that happens it can be hard to see what's happening in the present: if we're braced for trouble and distracted by memories, these old pains can stand between us as the world as it is now. You can use beryl in any form to help with this: centre yourself in the present moment, relax into simplicity, and open yourself to the growth of new possibilities. Beryl, spiritually, can soften our scars and let us move more freely again.

# Bloodstone

**COLOUR** green/red

**PATTERNING** dark, opaque green with red flecks

**INTERNAL STRUCTURE** hexagonal/monoclinic

**ORIGIN** Primarily India, though also Brazil, Western Australia, Russia, Europe, South Africa and the Americas

*A particularly dramatic variant* of chalcedony, bloodstone has a striking appearance, like green ground with blood speckled across it. It isn't a violent stone, though: what are we if not creatures of flesh and blood standing upon the green Earth?

What bloodstone brings to our energy is a sense of vitality and courage. It connects us to our physical bodies and our natural strength, grounding us so we can be who we are, where we are, as we need to be. Because of this earthy quality, this is a crystal that can be used as a talisman: bloodstone is strong enough to purify bad energy coming your way, not through quiet tranquillity but through the animal potency of something that knows its own worth and knows it has a right to stand in its own space. We don't have to do this selfishly; it's about being grounded in ourselves.

## Self-protection

Consider how the colours connect the root and heart chakras and you'll see how this works: we need connection and tenderness, and for this to be a source of empowerment rather than vulnerability we need to be secure and able to protect ourselves. This is a crystal where love comes from a place of strength: we know who we are and what we need, and when we understand that we will have the energy to be generous and big-hearted. It can even be a stone that carries us through times where we have to make sacrifices for those we care about: a bloodstone meditation can help you to find your limits, so you understand how much you can give today while remaining healthy enough that you can give again tomorrow.

# Calcite

**COLOUR** many shades

**PATTERNING** transparent to opaque, often forming points

**INTERNAL STRUCTURE** hexagonal

**ORIGIN** worldwide

*If you're looking for a mineral cluster,* calcite will be a good friend to you. It's a very commonly occurring crystal found in all manner of rocks, where it can act as a 'glue' when sedimentary layers are being created by the Earth; it is often seen as a vein running through other stones. This crystal is therefore easy to find – certainly in polished versions. It also frequently forms spars – so if you want a natural wand, searching for calcite is a good place to start.

The fact that it has so many variants also gives you a lot of choice if there's a particular colour you prefer to work with. Black and white calcite can be found, as can shades of green, blue, orange, pink, peach, red and purple: basically, there is no chakra that doesn't have a shade of calcite to match it.

## Amp up the vibes

Calcite's primary power is as an amplifier. It's a high-energy stone, and has a make-it-happen vibration that can be purifying in itself. This stone is particularly effective when you want to make a conscious decision on which direction you should point yourself. If you're developing an intention, calcite can help give you a push in the right direction, clarifying and powering up your own vitality.

From all this, the one take away you may notice is that calcite is a helper. It binds rocks, takes multiple forms, and shades itself from colour to colour, becoming whatever it can to fill the gaps the world leaves for it. There are two ways you can work with it. The first is to appeal to it to help you: calcite can be used to boost the energy you're sending out into the world. The second is to try to channel that pragmatic, can-do attitude into yourself: what can be done, and how can you be adaptable enough to be the one that does it?

# Carnelian

**COLOUR** red, shading through orange and brown

**PATTERNING** marbled and lightly translucent

**INTERNAL STRUCTURE** hexagonal

**ORIGIN** Asia, Europe, New Zealand, Canada, South Africa and South America

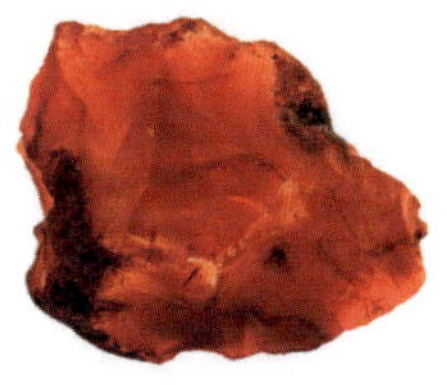

*Carnelian is a highly prized* and rather expensive variety of chalcedony, loved by jewellers not only for its deep colour and 'vitreous' (glassy) lustre but because it's a gift for the carver. This is a hard crystal that lends itself well to intricate designs, and it also gleams beautifully when polished.

The first carnelian mines were most likely in India and the Arabian Peninsula, and indeed, it's an ancient stone that has been honoured throughout history for its regal colour. Carnelian is a colour that invokes both flame and flesh. As such, it's a very physical stone associated with potent energy.

This energy isn't exactly a 'high'; rather, it's about coming from a strong source where you have everything you need. Carnelian is associated with the root and sacral chakras. If you need to feel secure in your body, it can be a powerful choice.

## Restoring your own faith

Carnelian is a grounding stone – and once you're grounded, it can dispel the fears and weariness that might be holding you back. It's a stimulating stone that helps you sharpen your wits and restore faith in yourself, a source of willpower and courage.

When mediating with carnelian, it can be helpful to feel out whether envy and insecurity are holding you back from being your best self. We all struggle with those feelings, but if they're dragging you down, carnelian can empower you to set aside thoughts of others and focus on doing what you do best.

---

**If you need to purify a crystal that shouldn't be washed or exposed to sunlight, putting it in the vicinity of carnelian overnight can be a safe choice to cleanse it.**

---

# Celestite

**COLOUR** varies, but frequently sky blue

**PATTERNING** transluscent, often found as geodes

**INTERNAL STRUCTURE** orthorhombic

**ORIGIN** primarily Madagascar

*While most of the crystals* we work with are hexagonal, celestite is orthorhombic, meaning that it's a dispeller of confusion. Its structure can amplify your focus as you seek to see through to the heart of things.

Celestite's best-known colour is a soft sky blue. This delicate hue makes it a stone that can settle your mind; as you seek enlightenment, you can do it from a peaceful place. It also connects to the throat chakra, which is a site of communication not just with others, but with yourself. The first step to insight is accepting the truth, and from there you can really see.

## Seeking insight

Celestite has a heavenly energy that is gentle, perceptive and calming. It's a particularly good if you're looking to deepen your mindfulness and insight. Spiritual seekers can use celestite as a crystal of enlightenment, opening up their awareness to divine vibrations and their hearts to wisdom. It can also come in the form of clear thinking and rational consideration: sometimes we need to apply our intelligence to a situation, and contact with celestite can help our ideas flow clean and precise so we don't get distracted by muddled notions or emotional hang-ups.

Social insight can also be a good intention with celestite: if you're seeking to understand others and really hear the truth they're trying to communicate, you can use celestite to open your attention and listen with unbiased patience and curiosity.

---

**Celestite is a great crystal if you want to do an exploratory meditation. While sometimes we sit down with a specific intention, it can also be good to just to let ourselves hear what the universe and our own psyches are trying to tell us.**

---

# Chalcedony

**COLOUR** a wide range of hues, especially white, grey, blue and brown

**PATTERNING** transluscent to opaque, sometimes banded, spotted or mottled, as well as being found in geodes

**INTERNAL STRUCTURE** hexagonal/monoclinic

**ORIGIN** widely distributed; major sites in Madagascar, Brazil and Western United States

*Chalcedony is one of those crystals* that can take many forms that are considered in a category in their own right: agate, bloodstone, chrysoprase, jasper and onyx) are all members of the chalcedony family. Seeing the underlying energy can deepen your understanding of each, and chalcedony is also available with its own identity, so it's worth exploring separately.

At a structural level, chalcedony has an interesting energy: it's the meeting of two different lattices. Like many crystals, it's a variant of quartz, which has a hexagonal lattice, but it also contains very delicate intergrowths of a mineral called moganite. Moganite is similar to quartz, but at a structural level it's monoclinic. What this means is that we have a close interrelationship of two different energies harmonizing together: the 'seeking' resilience of the hexagonal blended with the strong protective qualities of the monoclinic. If you need to explore something challenging, this can be a powerful combination: we can use it to reach out to others, and we can also use it to reach out to new thoughts and feelings.

## Speaking to others

One term for this crystal is the 'speaker's stone': its quality is to enhance thoughtful communication so you can reach out to others, whether it's making a speech in public or trying to make a personal connection. When we have things to say it can be easy to fall into being argumentative, sticking to what we feel is our truth and reacting to different ideas as if they were a threat to our identity. Invoking the energy of chalcedony can help us to a calmer state of mind, where we can say what we mean without fearing the words of others.

# Chrysoprase

**COLOUR** apple green, sometimes shading to yellow

**PATTERNING** sometimes translucent, sometimes marbled

**INTERNAL STRUCTURE** hexagonal/monoclinic

**ORIGIN** primarily Australia; also Brazil, Poland and Tanzania

*Chrysoprase is a variant of chalcedony,* and as such it understands the value of reconciliation at the molecular level. If you've been feeling low in spirit, this is a crystal renowned for its ability to heal the heart, steady the soul and lift you up to a place where the world feels warm and pleasant again.

It has a strong connection with both nature and the heart chakra, which is great for meditations where you give some space for feeling a past hurt with tenderness and giving it time to heal in comfort. Taking a lesson from the greenery of the living world, you can regrow if you give yourself a calm and healthy time, and allow your body and spirit to do what they were made to do – which is thrive.

## Divine love

Spiritually, there's an association with the divine aspects of love: we are part of a greater whole, we are embraced by it, and to accept this is an act of grace. The energy of chrysoprase is one of fulfilment, where we can regain emotional balance and become open again to inspiration, creativity and happiness.

---

**The energy of chrysoprase is full of joy. It's a birthstone for May, and brings with it a sense of uplift and optimism.**

---

# Citrine

**COLOUR** yellow, shading from bright gold to tawny brown

**PATTERNING** transparent, often occurring as points or geodes

**INTERNAL STRUCTURE** hexagonal

**ORIGIN** Brazil, Madagascar, Myanmar and Russia

*Some call citrine the 'merchant's stone',* associating it with wealth, and its bright, positive energy means that this wealth can take the form of emotional and spiritual abundance as well as more earthly gain. Put simply, citrine enriches.

Naturally occurring citrine is somewhat rare, and a lot of what's sold as citrine is, in fact, heat-treated amethyst. Naturally occurring citrine tends to be lighter, have no white portions at its base and, in the geode form, have larger points. Whether the citrine is natural or treated, though, you can enjoy the same positivity: this is a crystal that works with the solar plexus to channel your personal power, your confidence and your drive to live a rich life – whatever your idea of a rich life might be.

## Bring on the sun

One quality that makes it valuable to a crystal practitioner is that it's one of those unusual stones that doesn't need cleansing: it doesn't retain negative energy. Bad things don't take hold within it and it keeps its own cheerful potency. Citrine can look after itself, releasing the negative and letting prosperity flourish, and that's an energy you can take into yourself, growing the boldness and enthusiasm you need to make it happen.

Citrine is very much associated with the sun, meaning that it's tremendously energizing. Think of how sunlight doesn't just give living things the power to grow, but can also bleach away stains, chase away shadows and make the world feel clean and new. If you need a stimulus for your spirits, citrine is a popular choice.

---

**If you're comfortable with it, heat-treated citrine is fine and it tends to be more affordable. If you want to buy natural citrine, do so from an ethical seller you trust to be.**

---

# Danburite

**COLOUR** colourless, or light shades of yellow, brown and pink

---

**PATTERNING** transparent to transluscent, often available as faceted spars

---

**INTERNAL STRUCTURE** orthorhombic

---

**ORIGIN** discovered in Danbury, Connecticut, USA; now mostly mined in Mexico as well as Bolivia, Madagascar, Myanmar, Japan and Russia

---

*Danburite has an orthorhombic structure* that makes it a clarifier, cutting through obstacles and clearing away illusions – but this doesn't mean it's a stone that deals with us harshly. The colour range appeals to a need to be helped with gentleness rather than force: danburite tends towards the more pastel hues, with shades that don't overwhelm the eye or the spirit but allow us to absorb the energy at a quiet pace.

Different stones may speak to different chakras depending on their particular energy, but what they all have in common is that they speak of enlightenment in a soft voice – which is sometimes what we need if we're going to hear it. This is a potent stone with strongly spiritual associations; it's one of the strongest vibrational crystals, but with a gentle energy that can resonate with us in times of powerful emotion.

## Bring on the sun

If you're grieving, struggling with resentment or bitterness, or feeling stuck in a negative mental place, danburite can meet you with compassion and help you move forward. The energy of danburite will help us towards self-improvement, be that of the soul, the intellect or in the decision to take action – and it does it by working with us with a spirit of compassion. For meditation or prayer it can empower you to transcend, rising above your troubles and seeing more clearly.

There are times when we need to cleanse ourselves. This isn't our fault; bad experiences and troubled emotions happen to everyone, but they can fill our minds like cobwebs and make it hard to remember what we once wanted our best selves to be. Danburite is for when it's time to shine a light, clear out the clutter and move forward.

# Diamond

**COLOUR** colourless, yellow, brown, pink or blue

**PATTERNING** transparent, usually cut into a faceted gem

**INTERNAL STRUCTURE** cubic

**ORIGIN** Australia, Botswana, Canada and South Africa; also lab grown

*The hardest mineral on the Earth* is a diamond, making it highly prized in jewellery. You may have a diamond engagement ring or family heirloom, but there's a good chance that otherwise the jewel may simply be out of your price range when it comes to crystal healing.

There are also particular ethical concerns, both about mining conditions and the trade of 'blood diamonds', which are sold to finance wars and violence. The good news is that if the energy of a diamond appeals to you, there are other choices. Their hardness also makes them invaluable in industry: research into human-created diamonds began in 1954, and now lab-grown diamonds are so good that it takes a professional to tell the difference. They're a great deal more affordable – and avoid the issue of funding conflict – and on the molecular level they're identical, so well worth considering. Basically, they contain the DNA of diamonds and the energy of human ingenuity, which are both fine things for the spirit.

## A clear purifier

Diamonds are a purifier of tremendous strength and clarity. Whether natural or lab-grown diamonds, both can inspire the same creative spirit and lively intelligence.

---

**If you were born in April, diamonds are your birthstone, but you may prefer a birthstone that has a similar energy but isn't an actual diamond. The alternative birthstone is usually called 'crystal' by jewellers, but in practice that means any crystal with a clear appearance and a purifying energy. Clear quartz can be a great alternative, or you might like something with a cubic lattice like fluorite.**

---

# Emerald

**COLOUR** green

**PATTERNING** cut into a faceted gem, the clearer it is, the more valuable; can also be bought for less unpolished

**INTERNAL STRUCTURE** hexagonal

**ORIGIN** worldwide, particularly Colombia; also Zambia and Brazil

*Emeralds are pricey,* and ethical sourcing can be a particular issue – they might have been funding a war. The good thing is that with such gems, you can ask for certificates that verify they aren't conflict jewels. If you like the energy of emerald but can't afford one, you may be pleased to know that it's a variety of beryl (see pages 64–65), and a cheaper variant might serve you equally well if you find the right match for you.

## Stone of love

The green colour of an emerald links it to the heart chakra: to hope, uplifted spirits and a celebration of life. One name for emerald is 'the stone of successful love'. This can be romantic love, so a union sealed with an emerald can make a happy home; however, love comes in many forms and emerald energy supports them all. It's a jewel of affection, loyalty and positive feeling, including the ability to accept ourselves – which, after all, is the foundation of a healthy affection for other people.

Emerald is also a stone of health and vibrancy. Its energy wakes up the heart, encouraging us to make warm connections with others, and it also wakes up the mind. This gem can enhance clarity and communication, bringing us from alertness into wisdom. We can consider the green colour as a reminder of the power of renewal: new seasons come again and the world blooms in beauty. Meditation with emerald can be great for new beginnings or refreshing your feelings in long-lasting relationships. Positive emotions are key to the energy of this jewel.

---

**Emerald is a birthstone for May, but if it's too expensive, uplifting chrysoprase is a more affordable option.**

---

# Epidote

**COLOUR** green, sometimes with shades of pink

**PATTERNING** transparent to transluscent; polished stones, often with variegation; also clusters

**INTERNAL STRUCTURE** monoclinic

**ORIGIN** Austria, Mexico, Mozambique, Norway, Russia and United States

*Here is a stone of development;* its name 'epidote' comes from the Greek word for 'increase', chosen because its crystals often have one side longer than the other. Epidote doesn't form to stay within narrow confines: it transforms, reaching out beyond its bounds.

This stone's transformative quality allies with its green hues and pink shadings in a way that speaks to the heart chakra, meaning that this is a crystal of emotional connection. You can use an epidote meditation to promote personal growth, feeling out what is in your heart and letting that experience guide you towards how you want to develop as a person. You can also use it to meditate on kindness, forgiveness or reaching out to someone in your life. Emotional abundance is the theme here: rather than staying trapped feeling the way you are now, you can summon up the power to make things better.

## Pairing with other stones

This energy of abundance can also be a way to invite new positive events into your life. Epidote is a good option for amplifying the powers of other crystals. If you've set an intention and want to develop it, pairing an epidote with your primary choice can add some extra energy to the process, sending it out into the world in a spirit of positivity and development.

For this reason, it can also be a good pick if you're trying to improve your understanding of a situation. Pair epidote with a stone that evokes clear thinking and meditate on them together; the manifesting power of the epidote can help to put you in a perceptive state of mind, processing your thoughts through a foundation of positivity so that you can come to the best conclusion.

# Fluorite

**COLOUR** many shades, including in the same crystal; often purple, green or yellow

**PATTERNING** transparent to transluscent; polished stones, often with variegation; also clusters

**INTERNAL STRUCTURE** cubic

**ORIGIN** primarily China and Mexico; also Brazil, Spain and Russia

*Fluorite is a mineral that contains a secret:* put it under ultraviolet light and it will glow like magic. It has even given its name to this phenomenon in 1852: Irish scientist George Gabriel Stokes described it for the journal *Philosophical Transactions*, calling it 'fluorescence'. The physical properties of fluorite have been teaching us new ways of seeing for a long time.

The lucky thing for crystal healers is that, as well as being beautiful, fluorite can teach us to be safe and clear-headed. Its energy is orderly and calming; if things are spilling out of control or growing in the wrong direction, fluorite can help you identify and send your intentions out to steer them back to where they should be. This is why it's also good for creating mental clarity if your thoughts are all over the place: fluorite tidies us up. When there are things that are tangled, disordered and no longer helping us, fluorite is the crystal that can help us straighten them out.

## Return to self-trust

Fluorite is also a protector. Our first defender will always be ourselves, but if you're troubled with doubts, confusion and indecision, it can be hard to know what you should do for yourself. These doubts can come from within, but they can also come from other people; we've all met types who discourage us or make us question our own judgement, and they sap our energy dreadfully. If you're feeling manipulated or put down, a meditation with fluorite can remind you that you're a capable and sensible person who should be free to listen to their own thoughts and feelings. We can't stop the negative energies of others, but we can cleanse it from our minds and return to self-trust.

# Garnet

**COLOUR** mostly red, but also shades of green, black, brown and yellow

**PATTERNING** lustrous; sometimes clear and cut as a gem, sometimes opaque

**INTERNAL STRUCTURE** cubic

**ORIGIN** Asia, Australia, Brazil, Kenya, Madagascar, Mozambique, Namibia, Russia and United States

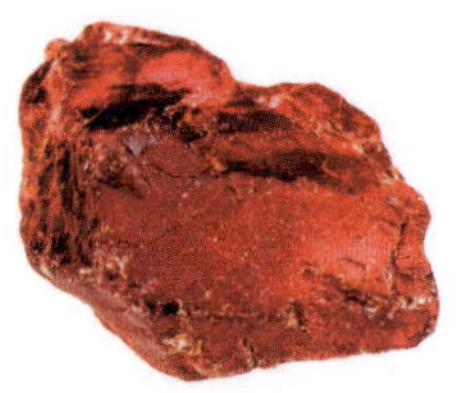

*Garnet is a gem found in antique jewellery* from cultures across the world; it's one of the longest-celebrated beauties produced by the Earth. Its cubic (isometric) molecular structure makes it a steadying force: garnet may look dainty as a jewel, but it's very reliable. Think of it like a psychological handrail – obviously it can't go out and solve your problems for you, but you can hold it when you need to stay strong and remember that you are capable enough to get through whatever you have to face.

## Fortifying energy

The beauty of garnet has endured culturally – and that's appropriate, because the energy of garnet is that of a fortifier. It has a strong connection to the root chakra, making it a crystal of vitality, life force, sexual potency and health. It can also be a good friend in a time of crisis. Garnet is for when you need to ground and re-energize yourself, allowing your spirit to get a firm hold within your body and take up all the space it needs.

The power of a garnet, then, is as an activator. It does this harmoniously, bringing your natural self into balance in a kind of primordial innocence: you are who you are, and you get to glory in it. With this as your foundation, garnet can be a great stone to use in times of change or new beginnings. It can also be a good stone to power up your intention setting: garnet is warming like a fire, and when it's time to get ready and meet life head on, this may be just what you need.

---

**Being that garnet is also the birthstone for January, it's well worth considering both for January babies and people looking for new starts.**

---

# Hematite

**COLOUR** silvery black

**PATTERNING** opaque with a mirror-like shine

**INTERNAL STRUCTURE** hexagonal

**ORIGIN** worldwide, especially Brazil, Canada, United States and Venezuela

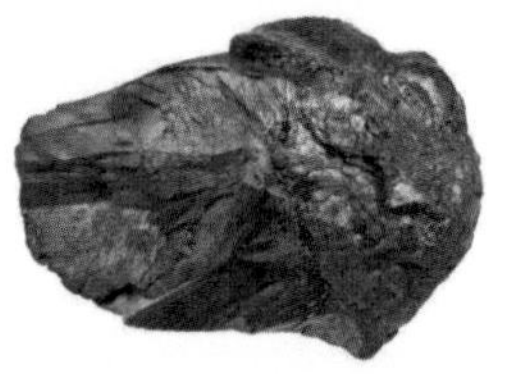

*Hematite is a combination* of deep black and gleaming silver that's quite extraordinary to reflect upon – and that's appropriate, because mental clarity is one of the things it's good for developing.

When wearing hematite next to your skin it has a rather wonderful quality: it's amazingly responsive to temperature. Put on some hematite beads and for a few seconds they'll feel freezing, but wear them for a minute and they'll have absorbed the heat of your body, radiating it back and keeping you toasty.

As hematite reflects, so can you, and its potent spirit will allow you to dismiss illusions and see through clearly to the heart of things. This is a grounding stone and a protector. Its energy is strong and harmonious; if you need to plant your feet firmly on the ground, the vibrations of hematite are excellent to invoke.

## Reflecting yourself

Hematite is a responsive stone, giving back to you what you put into it and reminding you of what you carry within yourself. It will work with you to create a shield that's powered by your own energy, holding it for you so you won't forget it's there if you need to face the negative energies of others.

You can also use hematite as a place to put bad feelings: send the toxicity and stress into the hematite, where it'll be held safe and reduced to nothing but a warm feeling you feel against your touch. You can cleanse the stone later – but it'll cool by itself too. Hematite holds no grudges.

---

**If you're on a budget, hematite tumbled stones are easily obtained and not too expensive, and the high gloss of the crystal will serve you well if you want to do some scrying.**

---

# Howlite

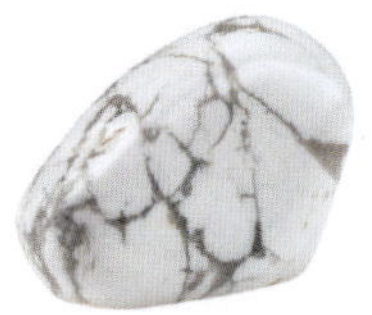

**COLOUR** naturally white and grey; also sold dyed

**PATTERNING** marbled and veined

**INTERNAL STRUCTURE** monoclinic

**ORIGIN** discovered in Canada; now also mined in Austria, Brazil, France, Italy and the United States

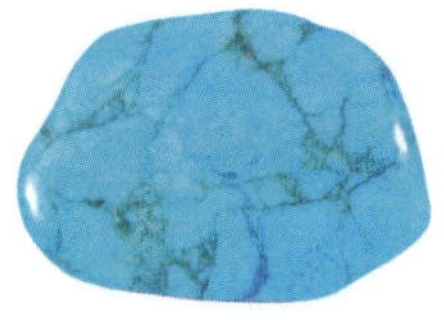

*Due to its paleness,* howlite takes dye well and is therefore sometimes sold as a different colour. Its veined appearance is like that of turquoise, so it is often dyed a similar blue. The dye doesn't affect the molecular structure within the crystal, but some feel that its vibration and power are affected nonetheless. This doesn't render it worthless; it's still powerful, just perhaps with a different 'flavour'. Decide whatever works for you; it's a stone of forgiveness, so we may take from it the lesson that everyone can shape their own individual practice.

## Path to meditation

Howlite is a stone thought by many to open a link to the divine. Your own experience of the divine will vary according to your own spirit, life experiences and culture, of course, but it is a stone that can be used with a prayer or meditation to open up the path and see what you learn.

The best way it can help you there is this: howlite is a stone of patience and calm. Others can anger us, and sometimes we have to stand up for ourselves or those we love; if we hold onto that anger when we no longer need it, it will close off our spirit from a wider world. Howlite's energy is about tolerance and understanding, a state of mind where we can reach acceptance and release the emotions that might be holding our souls back.

---

**Its gentle vibration can make howlite a good stone for peaceful sleep. If you're using a crystal for insomnia, make sure it's safely stored so it doesn't get lost or damaged overnight, but placing it near you can help you find rest.**

---

# Iolite

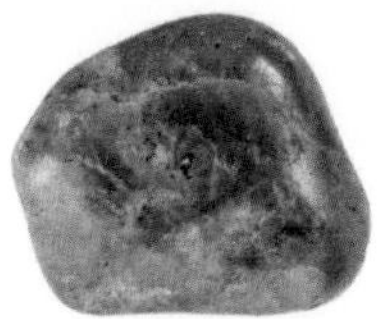

**COLOUR** violet-blue, sometimes shading to brown or grey

**PATTERNING** sometimes clear and sold as a faceted gem, sometimes marbled

**INTERNAL STRUCTURE** monoclinic

**ORIGIN** Brazil, India, Kenya, Norway, Madagascar, Myanmar, Sri Lanka and Tanzania

*Within its depths,* iolite has a particular secret – a geological phenomenon known as pleochroism. This is an arrangement of molecules that show different colours when seen from different angles, though this may not be so apparent if you have a rough gem. If you decide to splash out and buy a faceted jewel, expect to pay more for the jeweller's skill: iolite is tricky and doesn't give up its loveliest hues to someone who doesn't cut with a careful understanding of its inner structure. Having said that, you don't have to pay top price for the stone's insight: an uncut gem holds the same wisdom as a cut one.

## Opening up creativity

Iolite's colour links it to the third eye chakra, the site of insight and imagination; it opens us up to perceptual leaps, so no wonder iolite is a stone powerfully associated with vision and inspiration. It's a good helper for an artist or a spiritual seeker.

The pleochroism structure within iolite can bring a quality that's your friend when it comes to expanding your inner vision. Your own insights and creative leaps, too, are beautiful when they find the right light to shine in, but they are not to be shaken out of you by just anyone. Iolite is a guide to treat your third-eye self with respect; you can use it for meditations, not just when you're seeking ideas but as a way to reflect on what actions and surroundings bring out your most inventive and perceptive side.

---

**There's a story told about this stone: iolite is strongly associated with water, and at least some researchers believe that the legendary 'Viking compass' was an iolite stone that could show the direction of the sun on a cloudy day when navigating across the ocean. Indeed, iolite is a guide.**

---

# Iron pyrite
## 'Fool's Gold'

**COLOUR** dull gold

**PATTERNING** reflective, forming geometrical shapes

**INTERNAL STRUCTURE** cubic

**ORIGIN** widely found, especially in China, Italy, Peru and Russia

*You may know this mineral* as a bit of a trickster – it can be mistaken for gold based on its metallic lustre – but it's far from mischievous. On the contrary, it has a strongly protective energy that can keep you shielded during difficult times, a venerable guard dog of a crystal. On a cellular level, pyrite is a form of iron sulphite, with the elements iron and sulphur uniting to create it. Both are potent energies with a long tradition behind them: iron is lucky and repels hostile spirits, while sulphur is purifying and soaks up negative vibrations. In pyrite the two have combined, and in this we can see something remarkable – because pyrite is more friendly to the touch than either.

Iron has been used to make tools for millennia, but it rusts in the face of water and salt, two substances the human skin naturally produces. Sulphur, meanwhile, is brittle and known as much for its bad smell as its brilliant yellow hue. Both have tremendous energy, but neither really lends itself to prolonged handling. Pyrite, on the other hand, is strong enough to scratch glass, yet it holds its integrity in the palm of your hand. It's a union of ancient forces working in a transformative alliance.

## Encouraging personal identity

The gold hue links pyrite to the solar plexus chakra, the site of personal power and identity. In this resonance we can see its capacity to attract abundance. This can be external, but it can also be a sense of abundance within yourself, a knowledge that good things can come both to and from you. It glimmers, confident in its own beauty, and it holds within it a clean and steady force; if those are qualities you want to cultivate, try meditating with pyrite.

# Jade

**COLOUR** traditionally green, but can come in almost any shade

**PATTERNING** mottled or transluscent

**INTERNAL STRUCTURE** monoclinic

**ORIGIN** jadeite, primarily from Myanmar; Chinese jade is nephrite

*Jade consists of two very similar stones:* jadeite and nephrite. Of the two, jadeite is rarer and harder with a more translucent quality; nephrite is tougher and less brittle. However, these two are close enough that the difference was only discovered in the mid-19th century by the French mineralogist Alexis Damour. As their resonances are also very similar, they are covered here together.

Jade has a grand and ancient cultural history, being highly prized for its beauty, the detail with which it can be carved, and its harmonious resonance. You can find examples of jade in antique carvings down the centuries; there are even Stone Age tools that made use of it. Jade and humans have been working together for a very long time; we are old friends.

## Tranquil energy

This stone has long been associated with good luck and positive emotion, and above all with wisdom. Because jade comes in a wide range of colours, it's a flexible stone when it comes to working with different chakras. You can find jade in almost any hue if you're lucky (though rare colours such as lavender and blue may be especially expensive), so there are many options when you need to approach a chakra with wise thoughtfulness and peaceful care.

It's the tranquil and auspicious energy that unites all forms of jade, so you'll be bringing a similar underlying vibration whatever colour you use. This is good news if you're having difficulty sourcing a particular colour: if you want to bring jade energy to, say, your throat chakra but can't get hold of a piece of blue jade within your price range, it's perfectly possible to pair jade with another crystal such as aquamarine or blue lace agate and channel them together. Jade knows how to cooperate.

# Jasper

**COLOUR** multicoloured

**PATTERNING** opaque, often with bands or rounded blooms

**INTERNAL STRUCTURE** hexagonal/monoclinic

**ORIGIN** Australia, Brazil, China, Europe, India, Madagascar, Mexico, South Africa and Uruguay

*Jasper is an opaque variant* of chalcedony, but it contains a higher number of mineral impurities. This makes it both solid in appearance and prone to marvellous and dramatic variations in colour and pattern. Jasper is called the 'supreme nurturer'. By its very nature it embraces imperfection; however fantastical its beauty, its energy is earthy and deeply stable, holding you steady.

**Brecciated jasper** is made up of fragments of stone that have geologically bonded, often found in earthquake zones where the Earth has bound itself back together – an image of reconciliation and healing if ever there was one.

**Picture jasper** has in it shapes that look to the human eye as if nature painted a landscape – a sign of the Earth's bounty, and a reminder of the human capacity to find meaning in the world.

**Porcelain jasper** is intricately detailed, a stable stone that helps with balance and harmony.

**Orbicular jasper** contains colourful circles, an image of watchfulness against harm.

**Ocean jasper** carries the healing energies of the sea.

Jasper is a grounding stone, linking us to Mother Nature and nurturing us. The pieces that speak to you will be as unique and individual as you are. There is an energy of deep acceptance that we can keep by us in times when we fear that we're not good enough. Jasper is a reminder that when we embrace our flaws, love the differences in others, and let ourselves blend with the unexpected, we can become more vibrant and spectacular than if we'd strained to be perfect.

# Jet

**COLOUR** black

**PATTERNING** dullish and opaque, but can be polished to a low gloss

**INTERNAL STRUCTURE** organic

**ORIGIN** China, England, Siberia, Spain and United States

*Jet isn't a true crystal* but fossilized wood from prehistoric trees. These were ancestral trees, species that are now extinct and preserved in this dark and enticing gemstone. This is a gem that once literally lived; it stood under the same sun we do and absorbed its light to grow tall and strong. Then it became driftwood, travelling the ocean before finally joining the long journey into stone. It has endured and strengthened, and it will be there as you do the same.

## Shield against darkness

Jet is a spiritual protector with a talismanic power. As creatures adapted to live in the daytime and fearful of nocturnal predators, it's natural for us to fear the darkness; jet shields us against it. If you're setting out on a journey, be it physical, emotional or spiritual, jet can come along as a guardian.

Like other dark crystals, jet has the potential to be used for scrying. When you have a quest to undertake, gazing upon a polished piece can make an effective 'show stone': let your sight rest and your mind be open, and see what your vision suggests.

For similar reasons, jet can be good if you're trying to break a bad habit. Always be gentle with yourself when doing this; our psyches respond much better to patience than to punishment. You can use jet to protect yourself against self-blame as much as against the unwanted habit itself.

---

**There's a legend that all jet is from trees that were the same as the modern monkey puzzle tree, but in fact palaeobotany doesn't back this up. These were ancestral trees, species now extinct preserved in this dark and enticing gem.**

---

# Kyanite

**COLOUR** mostly blue and white, but can be yellow, orange, green or black

**PATTERNING** striated, often in a natural 'blade' shape; also cut into a faceted gem

**INTERNAL STRUCTURE** triclinic

**ORIGIN** Kali Gandaki region of Nepal and Tibet, Austria, Brazil, Kenya, Myanmar, Switzerland, United States and Zimbabwe

*Kyanite has an unusual quality* in crystal healing: it doesn't hold energy. You won't need to cleanse it because any negativity it encounters simply passes through it; kyanite remains quiet, tranquil and uncontaminated. This quality makes it a very good spiritual transmitter – nothing you send through it will get scrambled. If you need to take some time to sort things out in your mind, your intentions will come out clean and clear. It's just you and a pure space with no interference.

## Holistic healer

Being a crystal of meditation and insight, kyanite has connections to the third eye chakra, but it's also particularly good if you want to wash energy through yourself and experience all your chakras in harmony. Its clarity and neutrality can help them all flow together, everything settled and calm according to its own distinct nature. Sometimes we need to work on a particular feeling or intention and sometimes we need to experience ourselves as a holistic whole; kyanite is a particularly good friend to the latter.

Serenity is the vibration we take most from kyanite, which makes it a healer. Overstimulation can stress out the brain and overstrain can damage the body; we need to rest and take time to recover. A meditation with kyanite can be great for this, allowing you to experience a moment of silent ease in which you can release your tensions into an atmosphere where they will be gently dissipated, leaving nothing behind but your healthier self.

---

**Be aware that kyanite is rather brittle, so handle it with care. It respects the nature of others and can be well preserved when we do the same.**

---

# Labradorite

**COLOUR** blue and grey, sometimes shading into yellow

**PATTERNING** iridescent, translucent with a reflective sheen

**INTERNAL STRUCTURE** triclinic

**ORIGIN** Canada, India, Madagascar, Russia and Scandinavia

*There is a mystical beauty* connected to labradorite: turn it and you'll see it shimmer. This is an energy that connects us to the stars and moon, to the night-sky aurora borealis, a radiance in the palm of your hand. In essence, labradorite can bring us light, an energy you can use in a variety of ways.

If you're seeking spiritual enlightenment, labradorite has a strong connection to the third eye chakra, the site of visions. You can use it in a ritual to channel cosmic energy, or in a more free-form meditation in which you open yourself up to whatever comes. Labradorite can bounce back negative forces with its mirror-like gloss, reflecting into you only the bright and the good.

## Heavenly connections

It is a stone that speaks to the higher self, which can help nurture creativity. Think of it being like stargazing: when beginning an artistic idea, we are 'in the dark', not knowing what we want to create, gazing into that empty-seeming space until we spot the little glimmers and see the constellations they shape. With its connection to the heavens, labradorite can be a fine inspiration.

If you're going through a difficult time, a meditation with labradorite can help you connect to the deep universe and refresh your trust in its abundance. Problems can feel overwhelming, and you should treat yourself with compassion, but we need to remember the light and resist despair – you never know what might shine out of the shadows.

---

**This is a crystal that can be a good companion if you set an intention before you sleep to listen to what your dreams are telling you, or you keep a dream diary to track the murmurings of your unconscious.**

---

# Lapis Lazuli

**COLOUR** deep blue

**PATTERNING** opaque; often flecked or streaked with white or gold

**INTERNAL STRUCTURE** lazurite is isometric, calcite is hexagonal and pyrite is cubic

**ORIGIN** Afghanistan; also Chile, Myanmar, Siberia and United States

*Lapis lazuli isn't a crystal;* it's a metamorphic rock. This means that it began life as a different kind of stone but was transformed through massive heat and pressure. It was originally a variety of different stones, normally including blue lazurite, calcite and pyrite along with other mineral traces, all blended together to create its depth and richness.

Spiritual journeys are an important aspect of lapis lazuli. It has long been a friend to artists, prized in the Renaissance for its ability to make, in powdered form, a shade of blue deeper than any other, evoking religious mystery and the glory of the ocean. It can help you shed illusions, remaining clear-sighted and aware as you align yourself with an ever-emerging truth.

## Unlocking transformation

This truth aspect can also be a good ally if you have something to communicate: it connects to the throat chakra and can help if you have to speak in public or reach out in kindness to someone you've had difficulty understanding. It's an expressive stone, and the expression it supports is non-confrontational and constructive, bringing differences to a place of meeting.

Transformation is in lapis lazuli's very nature, and for this reason it's a stone with deep association with the spiritual, the esoteric and the higher faculties. If you're pursuing mysteries or deepening self-knowledge, lapis lazuli can be a key that helps you to unlock them: you'll have to find your own way of turning the energies it channels, but it will be there to remind you that change can lead to extraordinary beauty.

---

**Lapis lazuli is a somewhat porous stone, meaning that it is easily scratched, so wrap it up to store it safely.**

---

# Magnetite / Lodestone

**COLOUR** black, silvery grey, sometimes slightly rusty brown

**PATTERNING** a metallic sheen, sometimes in faceted crystals or grainy

**INTERNAL STRUCTURE** monoclinic at room temperature; cubic at extremely low temperatures (below -244°F/ -153°C)

**ORIGIN** Austria, Canada, Finland, India, Italy, Mexico, Romania and United States

*First, let's distinguish between magnetite* and lodestone: these are the same stone in two forms. Magnetite is an iron ore; lodestone is the same thing but with polarity – that is, it attracts and repels like a magnet. All magnets will be drawn to magnetite, but lodestone has its own charge whether there's another magnet involved or not.

Another curious quality is that this is a crystal, but what kind of crystal depends on how cold it is. Any magnetite or lodestone you encounter will normally have a monoclinic structure, but at temperatures below 120 K (around −244°F/−153°C), its molecules make a sudden transition into a cubic lattice.

Of course it's highly unlikely that you will encounter such temperatures, but it does speak to the dynamic power of this crystal: it's one that engages with the world in a unique way. When things get truly extreme around it, it regroups into the most sturdy and resolute of all configurations.

## Magnetic direction

This is a crystal that has been guiding us for centuries: the first magnetic compasses were made of lodestone. Magnetite will let us know, quite literally, where we stand. This is a grounding stone, one that can realign our energies so that everything within us is pointed in the right direction.

---

**If you have anything that might be affected by magnetism, be aware of that, and be aware too that this stone might attract small metallic grains. This is fine in itself, but it might make it more abrasive than you realize, so don't keep magnetite with other crystals or on delicate surfaces.**

---

# Malachite

**COLOUR** deep green

**PATTERNING** ornate and distinctive bands and rosettes in shades of green

**INTERNAL STRUCTURE** monoclinic

**ORIGIN** Australia, Congo, Gabon, Mexico, Namibia, Russia and Zambia

*The bold and dramatic patterning* of malachite makes it one of the most popular and striking of crystals; a good piece can be a real show-stopper. If you're looking to strike out for bold new ground, whether practically or spiritually, this is a good stone for you.

The green colour of malachite links it to the heart chakra, and there are few crystals in the world more unapologetically, vibrantly green than this. The heart chakra is about love and emotional connection – not just romantic love, but the tenderness that we feel towards humanity and the world as well as ourselves. Sometimes that's a soft emotion – but it's also the foundation of our strength. Without a loving heart, we don't sustain.

## Protective love

The power of malachite is a love that protects and stands strong. If you're striking out into the unknown, be it a journey, a life change or an emotional challenge, look to malachite to be on your side. If you're having a hard time, then its vibration is stimulating, potent and good for clearing away troubles: it will give you the energy to be your own best protector, knowing that you are worth the trouble and have the stamina to do what has to be done.

The energy of malachite is transformative and protective. This is a vibration that will heal you with vigour rather than gentleness, giving you a pick-me-up and supporting you as you decide to do whatever it takes to bring yourself to a better place.

Malachite is a good stone to meditate on visually if you want to feel connected to nature, and when you do, consider what might be choking your roots or cramping your branches. What do you need to stand in the light? Malachite can help you feel strong and bold enough to take the action that will get you there.

# Moonstone

**COLOUR** shades of blue, white or yellow with pinkish gleams

**PATTERNING** transluscent with shimmers in its depths

**INTERNAL STRUCTURE** monoclinic

**ORIGIN** Sri Lanka; also Australia, Brazil, Madagascar, Myanmar and United States

*Moonstone is filled with energy.* It is often associated with new beginnings, and this is best understood as part of the lunar cycle. We may think that we can shake off all our issues, but it's normal to have periods of growth, stability and setback. The energy of moonstone will help us know that it's always within us to shine bright again.

## Suppporting in ill health

Healing is a powerful property here. For those of us in generally good health, periods of sickness and sadness lower us, but we can use moonstone to remind us the moon will wax again and we will shine clear. For others living with a chronic health condition, there's a different reminder: it may be that 'well enough' rather than 'fully well' is the realistic goal, but in such circumstances we need to be soothed and consoled – something moonstone supports.

When health is frequently poor, we can feel as if we've lost our real selves, the person we could be if we didn't have to worry about being ill. Some nights the moon will be deeply shadowed in darkness – but up there in the sky is its whole self, untouched by the darkness that seems so overwhelming to our own eyes. Moonstone is a reminder that your precious soul is always complete and more splendid than the troubles that might seem to obscure it.

# Obsidian

**COLOUR** black, or black with white fragments within; green, red and brown variants

**PATTERNING** deep black and glossy, sometime with white blooms

**INTERNAL STRUCTURE** amorphous

**ORIGIN** Iceland, Italy and United States

*If you ask a geologist,* you may be told something intriguing: obsidian isn't really considered a 'rock' at all. It's congealed lava, mixed in with microscopic fragments of crystal and rock to form a natural glass: something that once blazed, and then cooled so fast it didn't take the time to arrange a formal structure. In other words, obsidian has within its foundation the capacity to act fast, to assemble clarity and strength out of boiling chaos. You couldn't ask for a better protector.

There are several varieties of obsidian; the most famous variant is snowflake obsidian, which contains white, blossom-like patterns within the black. This can add a touch of complexity to its powers, invoking purification and the quiet calm of a winter night.

## Revealing your truths

Don't look to obsidian if you want to preserve illusions: its strength lies in its power of truth. In past times magicians and seers polished up discs of it to make mirrors, which they then used for scrying. You can get obsidian mirrors to this day, and if you're looking for a gazing glass, their black depths and high gloss can be a powerful tool for opening up your mind.

Remember when you are gazing into obsiadian that you're coming to the process as a seeker: this stone's nature isn't to confirm preconceptions, but to reveal from the depths and protect your spirit, helping to keep you safe enough to handle whatever bubbles up from your own private volcanoes.

---

**Obsidian breaks easily, leaving a razor edge, and in ancient times it was used to make sharp knives. This also means that when caring for it you should handle it with respect – you don't want to injure yourself.**

---

# Onyx

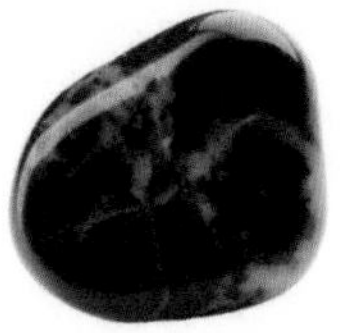

**COLOUR** black and white, but also comes in most colours

**PATTERNING** parallel bands of colour

**INTERNAL STRUCTURE** hexagonal/monoclinic

**ORIGIN** Brazil, India, Madagascar, Mexico, United States and Uruguay

*Onyx is a variant of chalcedony* that is similar to agate. The main difference is that where agate's bands are curved and sometimes irregular, the bands in onyx form a neat set of parallels. It has been long prized by jewellers on account of this, as the dramatic contrast made it an ideal stone for carving cameos.

This regular patterning makes it a particularly suitable stone for grounding you. Agate has steadying qualities, too, but onyx is particularly supportive if your emotions are disrupted or your life seems as if it's spinning out of control. This can be caused by external events that make you feel in need of extra protection, or it can be parts of your own nature struggling against each other.

## Bringing balance

Sometimes our different energies pull in different directions, and we need to take some time to let them each have their own space, express their drives and honour them in their variety. We can then set them in balance so that instead of working against each other, they can pull together. The parallel lines of onyx, setting brightly contrasting colours together in a neat harmony, is a good reminder of this goal.

Onyx is a stone of courage and good fortune – not rash bravado, but the courage of someone who knows who they are. Making a decision and sticking to it with stamina and fortitude can be tough; we stand the best chance when we have a clear sense of self and can reconcile our different needs and drives.

The stone can remind us that we never need to be one thing: we only need to accept that within our own complexity lies beauty. We can have mixed feelings and complementary sides to our character, and understanding this makes us stronger – once we know we can make it all work together.

# Opal

**COLOUR** any colour, usually a mixture

**PATTERNING** clear or slightly cloudy with iridescent flecks flashing within

**INTERNAL STRUCTURE** amorphous

**ORIGIN** primarily Australia and Ethiopia

*Opal is the chameleon gem,* shifting through a subtle range of colours and almost endlessly variable in terms of what you may find available. They're a birthstone for October and popular with jewellers for their beauty, so a really good one is likely to be expensive. In terms of budget, it's useful to know that opals can be classified as two types: common and precious.

Precious opals are those most likely to be set in rings and necklaces because they're spectacular: they contain what is known as 'play-of-colour', or the ability to shimmer different hues depending on the angle of viewing them. Common opals don't do this, but they can still be lovely and also hold the same energy.

## Bringing inner quiet

The energy of opal, like its colour, is all about the elusive and mysterious. This stone is associated with invisibility – not literally vanishing, of course, but with drawing yourself in so that you can avoid attention in times where what you want is quiet and privacy. And within that privacy, opal is also the stone of happy dreams, creativity and numinous insights.

What this means is that opal, like the colours within it, can teach us how to preserve our own inner space. Sometimes we want to stand out and be flashy; sometimes we have things to communicate; sometimes there are dangers to be braved or challenges to be faced. Sometimes, though, we want to be quiet and explore the world within ourselves – a deep and unbounded place where there are riches to be found. This is the energy of opals, so if you're interested, find one that speaks to your own secrets.

---

**Opals are particularly delicate stones, so avoid getting them wet and treat them with the care they deserve.**

---

# Peridot

**COLOUR** green to brownish green

**PATTERNING** opaque when raw; transparent cut and faceted gem

**INTERNAL STRUCTURE** orthorhombic

**ORIGIN** China, Myanmar, Pakistan, Tanzania, United States and Vietnam

*Peridot is one of the birthstones* of August, a cheerful green stone that can be found in high-quality jewellery as well as a more unpolished form. It's a little unusual among gemstones in that, where most can come in a range of colours, peridot can only be found in varying shades of green.

If you want to let go of negative energy and move forward, peridot is an excellent cleanser. Its colour has a strong connection to the heart chakra, especially as it's so resolutely green by nature: love and positive emotion are at its energetic core. It's a therapeutic crystal, one that will lighten your emotional burdens by letting you gently detach yourself from any jealousy, resentment or bitterness that are cramping your spirit. The vibrations of peridot are positive and happy, and they will gently encourage you to move into harmony with them.

## Expanding our world

This is a stone that can move you towards abundance. Peridot can be about literal good luck in your life – something it's always easier to spot and pursue when you aren't distracted by emotional baggage – and it can also be about what psychologists call an 'abundance mindset'.

A person constrained by fear or anger can think in terms of a 'scarcity mindset': there can only be so much happiness to go around, so any good things must be hoarded and any gains made by other people must be coming at your expense. The opposite of this sad and counter-productive attitude is the belief in abundance: that there can be win-win scenarios, that others' prosperity can enrich us, and that when we need the energy and confidence to do something, it will be there for us. That's the energy of peridot: it stops us starving our spirits and lets us expand into a welcoming world.

# Quartz

**COLOUR** a tremendous variety

**PATTERNING** clear, translucent or opaque, polished or naturally faceted

**INTERNAL STRUCTURE** hexagonal

**ORIGIN** primarily China, Japan and Russia; also Europe, Brazil and South Africa

*Quartz is almost a foundation stone* of crystal practice: it's a structure that can manifest in such a wide range of beautiful shades and shapes that a great many gems we treat as individuals are actually a variant of quartz. It's for this reason that it's worth giving it its own entry. Anyone interested in crystals will encounter quartz quite a lot, and they may come across curious or obscure variants they hadn't foreseen. It's good to know about its underlying properties.

Quartz has a hexagonal lattice structure (see page 13), meaning it's a crystal with 'seeker' vibration. This is a strong and naturally cooperative energy that will give you a safe and vibrant foundation to amplify your intentions. We can also see the cooperative quality of quartz in the very fact that it has so many variations. It may have a solid lattice, but quartz is flexible in how it expresses itself, scorning no expression and finding myriad ways to be beautiful. It's considered a 'master healer' crystal, the one that you really can't go wrong with.

There are so many kinds of quartz they can't all be covered here, but let's talk about some of the most important ones:

**Rose quartz** is one of the birthstones of October. A lovely, delicate shade of pink, rose quartz is deeply associated with love. In particular it's a stone of compassion: the warm, benevolent feeling you can hold towards both others and yourself that forms the foundation of a positive attitude. If you have suffered from an emotional knock, rose quartz can be an effective healer; forgiveness and recovery are strong aspects of it. You might also place it in your home in the hopes of attracting love; help it out by using it as a meditation crystal to foster a positive and generous attitude in yourself, because that's the energy that will draw love to you.

**Smoky quartz** is a November birthstone, brownish in hue with a translucent quality as if foggy within. This actually makes it an effective cleanser: smoky quartz knows how to purify, as the 'smoke' of life can be held within it and come to no harm. Its colour connects it to the root chakra, the place where our most primal needs for physical safety are held, so it's a solid choice if you want to ground yourself.

**Clear quartz** is colourless and transparent, almost glassy, though it can have attractive little 'flaws' running through it that add some texture. It's a wonderful purifier that is great for any kind of healing, as well as an effective partner if you want to amplify the energy of another crystal. Clear quartz is also particularly worth mentioning if you have an April birthday: the traditional stone is diamond, which is both extremely expensive and often unethically traded; 'crystal' is recommended as an alternative, and clear quartz can be a great choice as it has a similar energy while being much more affordable.

**Tangerine quartz** has a deep orange colour that connects it to the sacral chakra, a sensual and vibrant energy that awakens the joy of life and a celebration of the body. It's worth adding a particular caution here: most quartz is fairly robust about getting wet, but the tangerine colour comes from iron oxide that can leech out in water, so keep it dry.

**Rutilated quartz** is a dramatic one: it contains fine 'rutiles', or needle-like spines, of titanium oxide. These aren't flaws; on the contrary, they're an effective booster to the spirit, making this a particularly good choice for meditation and moments of uplift. Rutilated quartz can clear a blocked soul, helping it to find its way back to its rightful path.

---

**Clear quartz is one of the stones that doesn't need cleansing and can cleanse other crystals if placed alongside them, which is an excellent quality to have around.**

---

# Rhodochrosite

**COLOUR** pink, sometimes shading into orange, striped with white

**PATTERNING** banded, sometimes forming faceted crystals

**INTERNAL STRUCTURE** hexagonal

**ORIGIN** primarily Argentina, Brazil, Canada, Mexico, Peru and South Africa

*Rhodochrosite is a fairly common mineral,* though more brittle than some, so if you own a piece you should treat it with tenderness and respect. This, in fact, is the great lesson of rhodochrosite. Its colour connects it to the heart chakra, the site of love – but love isn't always simple. If you're looking for a stone that can help you process the more challenging sides of that emotion, rhodochrosite can be a good choice.

A simple fact is that love means vulnerability. Sometimes we've been hurt in the past by someone who should have loved us better, or who used 'love' as an excuse to mistreat us. Sometimes we love someone who, for all their value as a human being, can be difficult or complicated. This takes a toll on the energies like almost nothing else: the heart chakra is the centrepoint of our energies, and as social animals we desire a loving connection like nothing else. When love is difficult, the world feels difficult.

## Choosing love

Rhodochrosite is a support in difficult times of love. Sometimes we need to recognize that things aren't right, and that justice demands that we take a clear moral line. Real love demands nothing less, be it love of your better self, love of another, or the pure love of truth and humanity. Sometimes we need to be gentle, ease our own aches by tenderness to ourselves, and love other people with compassion and forgiveness, seeing in them souls subject to the same fears and struggles that can burden us.

Which is the right choice, and when? That's a question to take into meditation or deep reflection, and rhodochrosite can be a helper. The balance of pink and white, love and clarity, is what vibrates with us at such times, reminding us that sometimes love isn't just a feeling, but an act of strength.

# Rhodonite

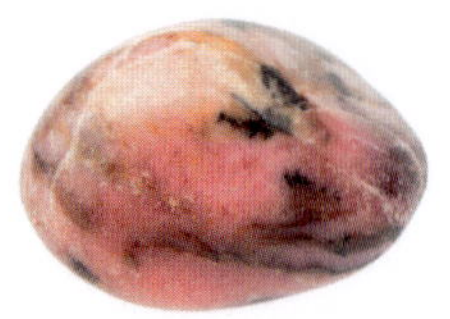

**COLOUR** pink and red shades

**PATTERNING** often speckled or veined with black

**INTERNAL STRUCTURE** triclinic

**ORIGIN** historically significant in Russia; also Australia, Brazil, Canada, Germany, Italy, Japan, Romania, Sweden and United States

*Rhodonite, with its deep, rose pink* and strong, grounding ornaments of black, is known as the 'rescue stone'. It's a stone of emotional recovery, of a heart that can survive.

In particular rhodonite is associated with what was traditionally described as the 'brotherhood of mankind', or, to put it in a more inclusive way, with human solidarity. This is a heart chakra stone: we simply don't do very well without love. Sometimes this is love for and from a particular individual, but it's also about the wider connection we feel with other people.

This is easier for some of us to feel than others. If we've been lucky enough to be raised by a supportive family and lived surrounded by kind friends, feeling part of the flow of humanity is easy and natural. In contrast, if we've experienced coldness, cruelty or the awkward pain of not fitting in, then that connection can feel out of reach, maybe even too dangerous to risk trying for.

## Opening up to tenderness

The truth is: it's lonely to feel alienated. Rhodonite can be a powerful stone if we want to cultivate our emotional resilience, helping us to warm the flame in our hearts that burns with unconditional compassion. Perhaps there is already a grand blaze, but even a tiny spark can grow to warm us if we let it have oxygen.

Try a meditation with rhodonite, imagining a feeling of positive, generous regard for other people. You don't have to think everyone's perfect and you don't even have to be social – you can wish people well from a safe distance if you prefer – but even that kind intention towards others can have a surprising effect. Rhodonite's tender colour can evoke gentleness and help us to start experiencing the healing that comes when we lay down our arms and let ourselves experience in safety.

# Ruby

**COLOUR** red

**PATTERNING** rough and opaque when unpolished; often cut to a clear, faceted gem

**INTERNAL STRUCTURE** hexagonal

**ORIGIN** traditionally India; more recently Afghanistan, Cambodia, Myanmar, Pakistan, Sri Lanka, Tanzania and Thailand

*Ruby, one of July's birthstones,* is a crystal of the kings. It's known as the 'stone of nobility' for the high prestige it enjoyed with rulers throughout history. Unsurprisingly it's associated with passion – that deep red hue – as well as prosperity, leadership, vitality and prowess. A really high-quality ruby can be even more expensive than a diamond. This may also mean that affording one might be a challenge – and as with any high-priced jewel, rubies may have been mined to fund conflicts, although a good jeweller should be able to certify a conflict-free provenance. If you can meet the high price and find an ethical source, ruby is a truly potent stone.

There are alternatives if you can't acquire a whole true ruby. Fragments of ruby can be found embedded in fuchsite or zoisite. Remember that you don't need a large stone to channel a crystal's energy: a small scrap will have all the power you need, and if you can't find one, fuchsite and zoisite themselves, being natural companions to ruby, can bring similar benefits. Another option is red spinel, which experts have had difficulty distinguishing from ruby until X-rays were invented in the 19th century. Spinel isn't the cheapest crystal, but it is cheaper than ruby.

Ruby is a gem that can be lab-grown. This is a personal choice – some people feel it's a fake, while others consider that it's the molecular structure plus the personal energy infused in it that does the good. Certainly, a 'synthetic' ruby is physically identical to a natural one, so if that works for you, it's definitely an option.

# Sapphire

**COLOUR** blue, but can also be pink, purple, yellow, orange or green

---

**PATTERNING** deep opaque blue when rough; clear and sparkling when cut into facets

---

**INTERNAL STRUCTURE** hexagonal

---

**ORIGIN** primarily Sri Lanka; also Australia, Cambodia, Madagascar, Myanmar, Tanzania, Thailand and United States

---

*A birthstone for September,* sapphire is one of the most valuable jewels in the world. As is always the case with such treasures, make sure to buy from a jeweller who can certify ethical sourcing. As is the case with other valuable gemstones too, you can source lab-grown sapphires if you prefer; on the molecular level they're identical to the ones produced by nature.

## Beauty in truth

The beauty of sapphires associates them with tranquillity, prosperity and wisdom Blue is the traditional colour, one that links particularly to the Throat Chakra and makes it a stone that brings out the beauty of truth, self-expression and communication. In fact, though, sapphires come in a wide range of colours; if you're considering the range, let your own instincts be your guide – a sapphire of any other colour is every bit as authentic.

An interesting variant is the 'star sapphire'. These remarkable crystals have a spray of light at the centre in a star-shaped formation, usually in 6 rays. It's a heavenly association with a potent spiritual energy. Being both striking and rare, they are unsurprisingly expensive, especially the high-quality ones – but the good news from a crystal practice perspective is that the 'star' is caused by rutile, the same needle-like mineral inclusions that create rutilated quartz. Both have a similar celestial energy, so if that appeals there is a more affordable alternative. There are also black star sapphires; their colour is caused by hematite, a powerful crystal you can get quite cheaply, so that's another way to get the same energy within modest means. You don't need a king's purse to enjoy a king's glories!

# Selenite

**COLOUR** milky white

**PATTERNING** translucent; often a pearly lustre when polished; can also form faceted spars

**INTERNAL STRUCTURE** monoclinic

**ORIGIN** Brazil, Mexico, Morocco, Poland and United States

*Selenite is a natural mineral,* and as a stone it has a soft glow that associates it with the energy of the moon: gentle, healing and mystical. This stone is lustrous when polished. It can also form natural spars, sometimes called satin spars, which have a more clouded, almost silky quality.

These spars can be good if you want a wand formation, as the striations form a quiet pathway to direct energies to flow the way you want. If your mood and psychological vibrations are all scrambled up, sweeping a selenite wand through your aura – about a hand's-breadth away from your body – can be a good way to cut through the negativity and feel clean again.

This is a crystal with a purifying energy that can leave you calm and soothed. The colour of selenite links it to the crown chakra, the site of transcendence and connection to the greater whole. This can be an overwhelming concept, but the energy of selenite is calming and helpful rather than dazzling, so if you want to explore that elevated side of your spirit, it can be a good one to start with.

## Airborne calmness

Because selenite is absorbent it is sometimes used to make essential oil diffusers. Be aware that a strong-coloured oil such as cinnamon may leave a stain. While this is fine if you don't mind, if you want to keep the crystal pristine, you should choose a less porous diffuser.

---

**Selenite is unusually delicate and easily scratched. Never put it in water, or even keep it in a bathroom – the moisture can affect it. Its energy is peaceful, so handle it with due respect.**

---

# Sodalite

**COLOUR** blue

**PATTERNING** marbled with streaks of white; opaque in large chunks, translucent in smaller stones

**INTERNAL STRUCTURE** cubic

**ORIGIN** Canada; also Afghanistan, Brazil, Bolivia, Greenland, Myanmar, Namibia, Portugal, Romania and Russia

*Sodalite is called the 'poet's stone':* its blue touched with white links it to the throat chakra with a glimmer of the crown chakra, and it can also have an indigo tone that invokes the third eye chakra. In other words, it's a stone that rests deeply in the truth, while also looking to the infinite.

The thing about a poem is that it can surprise us with a new way of seeing that brings together ideas we hadn't expected, but which feel perfectly right once we encounter them. That's essentially the energy of sodalite. It's a good crystal for working in groups; it can create harmony and help each person to bring out the best in the other. Communication couched in wisdom is the key here.

## Poetry of thought

It's also a stone that helps you create alchemy between the disparate parts of your own personality. We commonly think of rationality and instinct as opposite ends of a spectrum, but that really isn't so: both are methods of insight. We use rationality by conscious thought, and instinct by letting our unconscious processes take the lead, but they have this in common: they're about trying to see clearly. With both, our minds reach out to work at their full capacity, and when they do we get to see our knowledge in a clear structure. That shows us something we wouldn't have realized if we hadn't given ourselves the space to process it. That's the poetry of thought.

This is an energy that sodalite can help you access. A meditation with this crystal is about a search for truth – but it's a truth that you have to let yourself seek by using your own capacities. You are, in effect, 'writing' yourself, finding ways to make your intuitive perceptions and your logical brain rhyme together so that the whole they create is greater than each on its own.

# Spinel

**COLOUR** wide range of colours

**PATTERNING** transparent to opaque; forms natural crystals or is cut to faceted gems

**INTERNAL STRUCTURE** cubic

**ORIGIN** Afghanistan, Myanmar, Sri Lanka, Tajikistan, Tanzania, Thailand and Vietnam

*Spinel is growing in popularity* among jewellers, both for its beauty and its versatility of colour. It's a vibrant and dramatic gem with a truly striking appearance. Its cubic structure channels robustness, and this is the robustness of a character that knows how to win – and also how to be a good and kindly winner.

In terms of energy, it is best understood as a stone that enhances what is best in you. Its energy is about renewal: if you haven't been feeling your brightest, spinel's potency is there to refresh and revitalize you, reminding you of what is beautiful in yourself.

It's a stone that brings a positive attitude. This means more than hoping for the best or thinking well of yourself – though, of course, these are important aspects. It also means rejuvenating the parts of you that believe both you can succeed and you can carry a victory with grace, generosity and good humour.

## Pointing the way

It also has a secret trick: spinel is a little bit magnetic. The magnetism isn't tremendously powerful, and individual stones vary in how much of it they possess, but it is a stone that responds to the pull of the poles, especially the blue varieties. This is an energy that can help align you, pulling your own qualities together in a kind of psychological setting you straight, which can leave you heading in the direction you want to go. This does well with its optimistic energy: spinel can 'point the way for you' and encourage you to take the path to happiness.

---

**Spinel is one of the birthstones for August, and there are so many different colours that pretty much every mood and chakra will find a shade here that resonates.**

---

# Sunstone

**COLOUR** shades of red, pink, orange and yellow; sometimes green

**PATTERNING** transparent to translucent

**INTERNAL STRUCTURE** there are two varieties: oligoclase, which is monoclinic, and orthoclase, which is triclinic

**ORIGIN** China, Mexico, Madagascar, Namibia and United States

*Sunstone has a potent warming energy* that nourishes the spirit and encourages it to grow. Its energy is all about joy: the pleasure of living, the delight in yourself and the appreciation of others. It also has a couple of lovely tricks to it: aduralescence and aventuresence. Aduralescence is a kind of gentle, elusive luminosity, most famously found in moonstone, while aventurescence means having tiny mineral inclusions that glitter and reflect. In other words, sunstone is full of light – both soft light that gleams and bright light that sparkles. If you're feeling in need of a pick-me-up, you can't do better than a stone that gives you both.

## Breaking away

In particular, sunstone has the potential to help you detach yourself from emotional entanglements that can tamp your joy down. Sometimes people latch on to us, not because of healthy love but because they see our energy as something they can drain to fill their own needs. There's nothing wrong with generosity, of course, nor with caring for someone who genuinely does need to be helped; if they're kind, sunstone energy can help us appreciate what's good in them. However, if there's no celebration of who you are except in terms of what you can give, it's a relationship that will wear you out; it isn't sustainable forever.

If you're struggling to find your way through a situation like this, a meditation with sunstone can remind you how to feel joy in your own right. Unhealthy relationships can take up too much space in our heads, and the way to change this is to crowd them out with other, better things. Sunstone is about celebration, and you can channel that energy so you end up caring more about things that will make you happy than things that will drag you down. From here, your choices will be a lot freer.

# Tiger's Eye

**COLOUR** brown, but sometimes red or blue

**PATTERNING** fine iridescent stripes

**INTERNAL STRUCTURE** hexagonal

**ORIGIN** South Africa; also Australia, India and United States

*The gleam of tiger's eye* is one of the brightest of all the crystals, with a shine to it almost like polished metal. Its beauty makes it popular in jewellery while remaining fairly affordable.

The combination of shimmer and earth tones makes tiger's eye an energetic meeting point between the Earth and the sun. Its energies run a line through the root chakra, the sacral chakra and the solar plexus chakra, creating a sense of being grounded and confident in your own senses and appetites. This is a gem of authenticity, of innocent animal needs and the courage that comes from accepting them honestly.

## Charting your own course

The reflective quality of tiger's eye can invoke insight and spiritual uplift. This stone will allow you to feel your own power while also seeing the path you should take, which means it's a stone of action. If you're feeling indecisive, meditation with tiger's eye can shine a light.

Because of this, it's a good stone to use if you need to balance yourself. If you're mired in mundane hungers, tiger's eye will sympathize while helping you see a bigger purpose; if you're trapped in anxiety or guilt, tiger's eye can settle you into remembering your more earthy side.

The reflective 'eye' quality also makes it a good talisman for protection, in particular from the ill-meaning gaze of others. In many cultures the experience of being stared at is understood as a threat. Sometimes it's negative judgements from people who may go on to speak nastily behind your back; sometimes it's the envious stare of one who does not wish you well. Wear tiger's eye to deflect bad intentions while brightening your own sight so that it's you, not those who don't love you, that get to chart your own course.

# Topaz

**COLOUR** usually colourless, but can be yellow, brown, orange, pink, green, or shades of white, grey and blue

**PATTERNING** often transparent, especially as a faceted gem, but can be cloudy; more translucent than clear when unpolished

**INTERNAL STRUCTURE** orthorhombic

**ORIGIN** Brazil, China, Madagascar, Mexico, Myanmar, Namibia, Pakistan, Russia, United States, Sri Lanka and Zimbabwe

*There is a gentle abundance* to the energy of topaz. A whole rainbow of hues can be found in this stone, and even the way they manifest isn't simple. Its warmer shades can be created by chromium impurities, but it also has two distinct kinds of colour centres in its atoms: one kind reflects yellow-brown light and the other blue. Depending on how much of each is in play in a particular crystal you may have an artist's palette of different shades mixed in. Topaz is always open to wonders.

This is the energy topaz encourages you to open up to. It has the potential to work with all your chakras, and the vibration it brings is one of trust – in yourself and your own wisdom, and also in the world itself. There can always be good things, topaz reminds us. We can even see this in its birthstone status: it's one of the crystals of November, but blue topaz is also for March. It always has more to give.

## Finding positive energy

Topaz will promote an attitude of success, but this success is founded on empathy and relaxation. Sometimes we begin by feeling as if we already have plenty – if not in material terms, then plenty of good qualities and positive spirit. This is an attitude that makes it easier to be empathic towards others. Topaz encourages another vibration: it allows us to open ourselves up to the positive energy others put into the world. Topaz is a stone of nobility, and we are at our most regal when we know we should be proud of our 'kingdom' as well as ourselves – and our kingdom is the cosmos that we all share.

# Tourmaline

**COLOUR** almost any colour, sometimes two or three in the same stone

**PATTERNING** transparent when cut, sometimes with delicate striations visible; opaque or translucent when unpolished

**INTERNAL STRUCTURE** hexagonal

**ORIGIN** Brazil, Madagascar, Mozambique, Namibia, Nigeria and Zambia; also Afghanistan and United States

*One of the birthstones of October,* tourmaline is a stone of subtlety and variation, giving you range to expand into a fresh sense of self. One of the wonders of tourmaline is that it's strongly pleochroic – which is to say that the right stone can show different colours or shades at different angles, one often dramatically darker than the other. This is an image of the help it can give you, because tourmaline cleanses and will stimulate your chakras so that you can see things afresh.

Tourmaline is a potent and mystical stone that can support you when there's something in life that you want to gather your energies to manifest. The energy of tourmaline is that of an indicator: it clears away the clutter that stands between you and new ways of seeing. It's simultaneously grounding and inspiring: if you've got lost in your thoughts, been confused by deceptions or plagued by indecision, tourmaline will get you steady again, reminding you of how strong you can truly stand. With your spirit cleared of distractions and illusions, a new space can open up, and into it can flow insights, decisions and creative ideas.

## Bringing us out of ourselves

You can think of tourmaline as a crystal of transformation, not by coming in as an outside force but by bringing out what is already there. It can be good to meditate on when balancing disparate parts of your personality, dark and light, active and receptive, the different 'shades' of you that may sometimes feel hard to reconcile. Tourmaline reminds us that we can have apparent contradictions for a reason: life is never just one note. Different situations can call for us to bring different energies to bear, and it's always worth reflecting whether you might break through a challenge by engaging another side of yourself.

# Turquoise

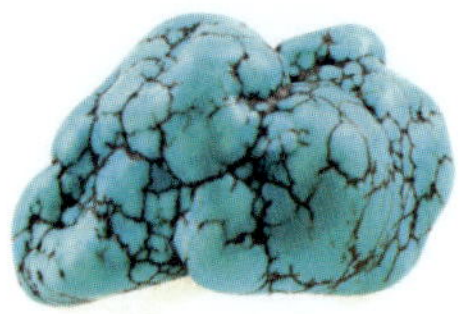

**COLOUR** distinctive blue tinged with green; also a rare yellow variant

**PATTERNING** opaque, often with dark veining

**INTERNAL STRUCTURE** triclinic

**ORIGIN** primarily Australia, Chile, Iran, Mexico and United States

*Turquoise has a long and noble history,* having been prized as a jewel and lucky talisman in many ancient cultures. Its energies are particularly associated with cleansing and purification, wellbeing and positive energy. The much less common yellow turquoise contains the same energy as the traditional blue one, but its colour is caused by the inclusion of iron. Iron is associated with good fortune and traditionally repels malevolent spirits, which is very much the energy of all turquoise, so if you come across a piece that appeals to you, don't let the different appearance discourage you! Blue may speak more to the throat chakra and yellow to the solar plexus chakra, but either way, your truth and your power will always ring in harmony.

The essence of turquoise is that it's a meeting place between the Earth, which cradles and formed it, and the sky, whose colour its own blue shade reaches out to greet. These aren't opposites when it comes to turquoise energy: rather, they're a complementary balance that cradles us. Without Earth, we have nowhere to stand; without sky, we have nothing to light our path. This is where turquoise leads us – into experiencing ourselves as a focal point of awareness between two mighty and benevolent forces.

## Balance and safety

In a spiritual and psychological sense, this duality in turquoise means that its energy is fundamentally one of both balance and safety. It is a place of healing, not in a quiet convalescence but in a dynamic experience where we are free to dream high and consider the bigger picture while remaining protected. Turquoise is a guardian stone for expanding our awareness, creating inner peace as we remain dynamic and engaged in the world.

# Zircon

**COLOUR** wide range of yellows, browns, greens, reds and blues; sometimes colourless

**PATTERNING** clear, faceted gems; untreated, sometimes a more cloudy appearance

**INTERNAL STRUCTURE** tetragonal

**ORIGIN** Australia, Cambodia, Sri Lanka, Thailand and Vietnam

*Zircon is an ancient crystal* that has been admired for its beauty for many centuries. This stone is from the neosilicate group, which also includes garnet and topaz. Sometimes it is heat treated to create more intense colours, but the same is true for many minerals.

This is one of the December birthstones. It's worth noting that colourless zircons can bear a very strong similarity to diamonds (see pages 82–83). If diamond is your birthstone, clear zircon might be worth considering as a cheaper alternative.

## Virtuous spirit

The vibrations of zircon are balancing, and in particular they're associated with virtue. When we're spiritually healthy it's natural for our virtuous side to be uppermost. This doesn't mean we're perfect, of course: we can experience anger, jealousy and so on, but we can also feel compassion, honesty and integrity as stronger motivators – and it's the latter traits that should guide our decisions.

The wisdom of zircon can help us with that: we may wobble this way and that, but we can come to our natural resting place, which is essentially good. In this way zircon can help us remember our best selves from day to day, meaning that we can keep in consistent touch with our most honourable intentions.

---

**Zicon is sometimes confused with cubic zirconia, but these have nothing to do with each other. The naturally occurring zicon belongs to stones in the neosilicate group, while cubic zirconia is a synthetically created gemstone, usually sold as a low-price alternative to diamond.**

---

# Zoisite / Tanzanite

**COLOUR** tanzanite is indigo blue; zoisite comes in shades of white, green, brown, pink and red

**PATTERNING** a clear gem cut to facets; also opaque and lustrous, sometimes with colour variations within a single stone

**INTERNAL STRUCTURE** orthorhombic

**ORIGIN** Germany, Italy, Mexico, Scotland and Switzerland; tanzanite is from Tanzania

*Some writers talk about this crystal* as zoisite, some as tanzanite, so what's the difference? Put simply, tanzanite is a variety of zoisite: discovered in Tanzania, it has a deep violet-blue shade that is particularly prized. All zoisite can be pleochroic – that is, different colours can be seen depending on which angle the light strikes it from – and tanzanite reflects its changes of hue with particular drama. Tanzanite is valued in fine jewellery and is therefore more expensive, but if the energy appeals, other varieties of zoisite will have a similar vibration (and can also be very pretty).

Many zoisites, especially tanzanite or other variants used in jewellery, have undergone heat treatment to enhance their colour. If you feel a particular resonance with such a stone, perhaps that's an image of how you'll work with it: sometimes there's a more vibrant beauty within, and it just takes a little energy to bring it out.

## Positive clarity

Regardless of the variant, the energy of all zoisites is about waking up your mind. It's a stimulating vibration that has a particular kinship with creativity, free thinking and emotional independence. This isn't about not needing or caring for others; in particular, a zoisite with a green or pink shade may speak directly to the heart chakra. Rather it's about the positive clarity that comes from understanding the good sides of yourself.

You can remain deeply connected to the world and other people – indeed, this may be one of those good points – but it's an energy that comes from within and holds its own integrity. It reaches for inspiration, spiritual connection, artistic insight and emotional health, and it does this by supporting you to be your own guide.

# Picture Credits

The publisher would like to thank Shutterstock and the following photographers for the use of copyright material: Africa Studio: 120 (top); AKaiser: 129; Albert Russ: 12 (left); AleksaStanko003: 45, 114 (top); Alex.K Photography: 122 (bottom); Anastasia Bulanova: 66 (top); Andriana Syvanych: 17 (foreground), 72 (top), 94 (top), 126 (top); ArtOfPhotos: 138 (top); aura23: 140 (bottom); Bjoern Wylezich: 50 (bottom), 120 (bottom); Black BW: 118 (bottom); Byjeng: 34 (centre); Cagla Acikgoz: 13 (centre), 88 (bottom), 114 (bottom), 150 (top); Dmivmas: 44 (top); Finesell: 58 (bottom); firdausrakaa: 136 (top); FotoHelin: 66 (bottom); galka3250: 34 (right), 35 (left), 36 (left), 110 (top), 116 (bottom), 122 (top); IamTK: 76 (top), 118 (top), 142 (top), 156 (top); Imfoto: 13 (left), 84 (top), 90 (bottom), 130 (top), 144 (bottom); J. Palys: 54, 116 (top); Jirik V: 152 (top); KaterinaSB: 64 (bottom); kongsky: 100 (bottom); KrimKate: 35 (centre), 96 (top), 98 (top), 124 (top), 124 (bottom), 154 (top), 156 (bottom); luca pbl: 146 (top); luchschenF: 82 (bottom); Mali lucky: 62 (top); Marco Fine: 62 (bottom), 98 (bottom); Maria Alam Sraboni: 52 (bottom); Marieke Peche: 106 (bottom); Marina Onokhina: 86 (bottom); Marykor: 33 (centre); Masianya: 130 (bottom); Mehmet Gokhan Bayhan: 47; Minakryn Ruslan: 48 (top), 68 (bottom), 70 (top), 108 (top), 146 (bottom), 148 (top); mineral vision: 52 (top), 55, 102 (top), 148 (bottom); Mineralsparadise: 64 (top); Mivr: 70 (bottom); Moha El-Jaw: 104 (bottom); MXW Stock: 92 (top); Nadin_T: 68 (top); NavMinerals: 110 (bottom); New Africa: 34 (left), 82 (top); ntv: 50 (top); Nyura: 36 (right), 94 (bottom); olpo: 76 (bottom), 78 (bottom); P. Qvist: 86 (top); photo-world: 84 (bottom), 134 (bottom), 136 (bottom); PhottoNZ: 140 (top); PNSJ88: 56 (bottom); Raymond.Evans: 90 (top); Richard Peterson: 74 (bottom); Sebastian Janicki: 12 (centre), 44 (bottom), 126 (bottom), 152 (bottom); sophiecat: 138 (bottom); Stellar Gems: 80 (top); Studio 888: 102 (bottom); TayHamPhotography: 72 (bottom); v_kulieva: 17 (background); vvoe: 12 (right), 13 (right), 33 (left), 33 (right), 35 (right), 36 (centre), 48 (bottom), 56 (top), 58 (top), 60 (top), 60 (bottom), 74 (top), 80 (bottom), 88 (top), 92 (bottom), 96 (bottom), 100 (top), 104 (top), 106 (top), 108 (bottom), 112 (top), 112 (bottom), 128, 132 (top), 132 (bottom), 142 (bottom), 144 (top), 150 (bottom), 154 (bottom); yul38885: 78 (top); Yut chanthaburi: 134 (top).

First published 2025 by
Ammonite Press
an imprint of Guild of Master Craftsman Publications Ltd
Castle Place, 166 High Street, Lewes, East Sussex, BN7 1XU, UK
www.ammonitepress.com



ISBN 978-1-78145-502-9



The EEA authorised representative is Authorised Rep Compliance Ltd.
Ground Floor, 71 Baggot Street Lower, Dublin, DO2 P593, Ireland
www.arccompliance.com

A catalogue record for this book is available from the British Library.

**Publisher** Jonathan Bailey
**Production Director** Jim Bulley
**Design Manager** Robin Shields
**Senior Project Editor** Tom Kitch
**Designer** Michael Whitehead
**Illustrator** Alejandra Penaloza
**Editor** Theresa Bebbington
**Consultant** Alexandra Garland

Color reproduction by GMC Reprographics
Printed and bound in China

To order a book, contact:
GMC Publications Ltd
Castle Place, 166 High Street,
Lewes, East Sussex, BN7 1XU,
United Kingdom
Tel: +44 (0)1273 488005
www.gmcbooks.com

AMMONITE
**PRESS**

**ammonitepress.com**